The Healthy Cookbook

Practical recipes with step-by-step instructions

STAR
FIRE

Publisher and Creative Director: Nick Wells
Art Director: Mike Spender
Project Editor: Cat Emslie
Editorial Planning: Toria Lyle
Layout Design: Theresa Maynard,
and Mike Spender and Colin Rudderham (original edition)
Digital Design and Production: Chris Herbert and Claire Walker

08 10 12 11 09

1 3 5 7 9 10 8 6 4 2

This edition first published in 2008 by
STAR FIRE
Crabtree Hall, Crabtree Lane,
Fulham, London, SW6 6TY
United Kingdom

www.star-fire.co.uk

STAR FIRE is part of The Foundry Creative Media Company Limited

© 2008 this edition The Foundry Creative Media Co. Ltd

ISBN 978-1-84786-190-0

The CIP record for this book is available from the British Library.

Printed in China

Authors: Catherine Atkinson, Juliet Barker, Gina Steer, Vicki Smallwood,
Carol Tennant, Mari Mererid Williams, Elizabeth Wolf-Cohen and Simone Wright
Editorial (original edition): Sara Goulding and Sara Robson
Photography: Colin Bowling, Paul Forrester and Stephen Brayne
Home Economists and Stylists: Jacqueline Bellefontaine,
Mandy Phipps, Vicki Smallwood and Penny Stephens

All props supplied by Barbara Stewart at Surfaces

NOTE
Recipes using uncooked eggs should be avoided by infants,
the elderly, pregnant women and anyone suffering from an illness.

Contents

High Fibre

Cancer Fighting Food

High Blood Pressure

Allergy Free

Wheat & Gluten Free

Dairy Free

Enjoying a High Fibre Lifestyle

Many believe the saying 'you are what you eat', and whether this is true or not there is no denying that a healthy lifestyle is vital for us all. A healthy lifestyle embraces diet (both food and drink) and exercise, two things that are essential for everyone, no matter what age group they belong to. Food and drink are required for survival and contain our bodies' building blocks. It follows that the healthier your diet, the better your quality of life, and in many cases the longer your life will be. It therefore makes sense that you look at your diet, and change or amend it if necessary.

Most diets tend to be high in refined foods such as white bread, white flour and processed cereals, from which natural fibre has been stripped. A diet low in fibre may lead to constipation or bowel disorders, but by increasing the amount of fibre you eat you may help to prevent these problems. A high fibre diet is therefore not a 'special' diet or one to be embarked on only on medical advice, but a way of life for anyone wanting to be healthy. Fibre provides the fuel for our bodies that keeps us going, giving us the energy not only to move around, exercise and work but also to repair the body and

grow. Deprived of this, the body will quickly start to break down.

Recently there have been a rush of popular diets, many of which have advocated reducing or eliminating carbohydrates, the source of all dietary fibre. This is a very dangerous way of eating. If the diet concentrates more on protein and fats there is the danger that, over time, vital organs begin to break down and life-threatening illness can occur. Fibre is vital to ensure the smooth running of the digestive system. It therefore cannot be stated too strongly that a well-balanced diet is essential for good health. As a general rule, the British Department of Health advocates that half the total intake of food should be carbohydrate and the other half made up of protein and fats. Unfortunately the reverse is true for many of us, which is when problems can start to occur. It is interesting to note that other countries advocate a different breakdown and recommend an even higher proportion of carbohydrate to fat and protein – the World Health Organisation, for instance, advocates a carbohydrate/fibre intake of between 55–75 per cent.

Energy consumed by us is calculated in kilo calories (often shortened to calories) and a certain recommended daily intake is advised by health experts, although it should be noted that the actual amount required by each individual depends on age, activity, the ratio of fat to muscle, and other factors such as being overweight, ill or fighting a disease. For people maintaining a reasonably active lifestyle the guidelines are as follows:

Men (aged 19–59) 2,550 kcal
Women (aged 19–50) 1,940 kcal
or (aged 51–59) 1,990

When trying to lose weight it is the fat that should be drastically reduced, then the protein. The carbohydrate

(especially in the form of fibre) should if anything be increased, but unfortunately it is the carbohydrate that is normally reduced. Most foods, with the exception of oils and sugar, are a mixture of fibre, fats and protein in a lesser or greater degree. It is therefore important that there is a greater understanding of what components are contained within the foods so that an informed decision can be made.

There are two main kinds of carbohydrates – starch and sugar. Starch carbohydrates are also known as complex carbohydrates and they include cereals, pulses, beans, breads, potatoes, pasta and rice. Eating wholegrain varieties of these foods will provide you with plenty of fibre. Sugar carbohydrates, or intrinsic sugars, are found in fruits and vegetables. These are 'good' sugars, as they still contain their cellular structure which, again, provides us with fibre. The extrinsic sugars, as found in sugar, honey, fruit squashes, cakes, biscuits and sweets, etc. are bad for us as they are refined, with all of the cellular structure removed. As a general guide, you should try to eat more of the following: wholemeal bread and pasta, brown rice, wholemeal flour to make pastry or homemade cakes and biscuits, wholegrain breakfast cereals, plenty of vegetables and fruit (especially oranges, pears, apples, avocados, grapefruits, prunes, berries, figs, pulses including baked beans, kidney beans and lentils, jacket potatoes, carrots, sweetcorn, broad beans, runner beans, peas and sprouts) and nuts such as peanuts, almonds and coconut. Always remember to drink plenty of fluids on a high fibre diet, as fibre retains fluid and you may become dehydrated easily.

Complex carbohydrates are a good choice for those concerned about weight gain as they are bulky and slow to digest, so will keep you feeling fuller for longer and reduce the desire to snack. These also contain minerals and vitamins and help the body conserve the benefits of any protein consumed. A further advantage is that, by eating a lot of fibre, the fat content of the diet is very much reduced and cholesterol levels are kept low. Eating high amounts of fat, especially saturated fat, has been proven to increase blocking of the arteries and lead to heart problems such as angina, strokes and heart attacks.

The best sources of fibre in our diet come from complex carbohydrates and come in two forms, soluble and insoluble. Insoluble fibre comes mainly from plants, and good sources are wheat, corn, rice, pulses and vegetables. The importance of insoluble fibre in the diet is paramount, as it helps to keep the intestines healthy and the digestive system in good working order. Fibre helps to prevent constipation and is believed to help in the prevention of bowel cancer. Soluble fibre is found in fruits, barley and rye and many believe that a good supply of soluble fibre helps to prevent LDL – the bad cholesterol found in blood.

It is generally recommended that 24 g per day of fibre is consumed to maintain a healthy diet, although it is estimated that in the west we consume only 13 g per day. Eating more will have untold benefits on your health.

The High Fibre section of this book (pages 18–57) contains recipes designed to increase the amount of fibre in your diet, whether you are doing it on medical advice or just because you want to eat more healthily. The recipes are delicious, easy to prepare and cook, and offer a broad span of tasty recipes that will appeal to all. From Mixed Grain Pilaf and Cream of Pumpkin Soup to Potato Skins and Oaty Fruit Puddings, you'll find something everyone will love whether they are following a high fibre diet or not.

Fighting and Preventing Cancer

It is an unfortunate fact that cancer is one of the most widespread diseases in the world. A vast amount of research has been done and is still ongoing into both the causes of cancer and what can be done to prevent the outbreak and spread of the disease throughout the body. Although we are still some way off a cure, there have been many breakthroughs over the last 30 years. Scientists now accept that cancer is often hereditary, but current research suggests that a very large contributory factor is lifestyle. With the increase of obesity we are seeing a substantial increase in cancer which can be linked to a bad diet. Other well-documented factors include cigarette smoking, lack of exercise and too much alcohol.

Cancer can occur in all parts of the body and starts as a rogue cell that gets out of control. Usually the body's immune system controls the growth of cells, but when the immune system breaks down, a 'rogue' cell can occur that starts to behave abnormally. Once the cell goes 'rogue' it can lie undetected for long periods before the growth becomes apparent, but by this time the damage has often been done. The rogue cell spreads throughout the body, embracing and changing healthy cells to form tumours, which can either be malignant (that without detection will spread throughout the body) or benign, which grow within themselves.

Preventive measures play a hugely important part in the fight against cancer. There is growing evidence that diet can and does play an important role in both preventing the development of cancer and helping to control it, so it makes sense, especially if you have a family history of cancer, to take note of your diet and if necessary change it.

Food is not only vital as fuel for the body but can also give the immune system that vital boost to help fight the disease. Health experts estimate that roughly one third of all cancers could be diet related. It is strongly advised that, alongside conventional medicine, a healthy diet, regular exercise and time for relaxation are important factors in both giving yourself the best chance of fighting cancer and improving your quality of life.

In the past, scientists researching cancer-related diseases have been puzzled as to why some countries have a far greater number of cancer sufferers than others. Now that the onset of many cancers have been so strongly linked to diet, it is easier to understand. In the East, where much rice is consumed with very little saturated fat and minimal amounts of meat, there is a far lower incidence of breast, stomach and bowel cancers. Their diet includes a large amount of plant foods containing fibre, as well as very low amounts of the fats and refined products that we eat in the West. The fibre consumed means that the food does not stay in the intestines long and so there is less danger of a build up of toxins.

It therefore makes sense to look carefully at diet in the fight against cancer, whether you are suffering from it or just concerned that you may be at risk. A very simple guide when

choosing cancer-fighting foods is to look for the reds, orange and greens and eat plenty of fruit and vegetables. Below are some of the best foods for a cancer-fighting diet in more detail.

Avacados are rich in glutathione, a powerful antioxidant that attacks free radicals. Free radicals are naturally produced by the body while producing energy. However if too many free radicals are produced (due to stress, smoking, pollution, the sun rays, illness, etc.) then they can cause cell damage which leads to cancer and other diseases. Avocados also provide more potassium than bananas and are a strong source of beta carotene.

Broccoli, Brussels sprouts, cabbage and cauliflower have a chemical component called indole-3-carbinol that can help combat breast cancer. Broccoli also contains the phytochemical sulforaphane, believed to help prevent colon and rectal cancer. All contain antioxidants that may help decrease prostate and other cancers.

Carrots also contain large amounts of beta carotene, which may help reduce a wide range of cancers. Falcarinol, also found in carrots, is thought to reduce the risk of developing the disease. They are best eaten raw for the most benefit.

Chilli peppers contain capsaicin, which may neutralize certain cancer-causing substances and help prevent stomach cancer.

Fish and shellfish, especially oily fish, rich in omega-3 fatty acids, should be eaten two to three times a week. Fish contains selenium as well as having no saturated fat.

Fruit is hugely important to any healthy diet, but particularly one that aims to fight cancer. Figs, grapefruit, oranges, lemons, grapes, papayas and all berries (especially raspberries, strawberries, blueberries and blackberries) should all be eaten regularly.

Garlic has immune-enhancing allium compounds that appear to increase the activity of immune cells that fight cancer and indirectly help break down cancer-causing substances. Onions, leeks and chives are good to include in your diet for the same reason.

Mushrooms appear to help the body fight cancer and build the immune system. They contain polysaccharides that build immunity and a protein called lectin, which attacks cancerous cells and prevents them from multiplying.

Nuts contain antioxidants and selenium, both of which are important in fighting cancer.

Soya products such as tofu contain several types of phytoestrogens that could help prevent both breast and prostate cancers by blocking and suppressing cancerous changes.

Sweet potatoes have many anti-cancer properties including beta carotene.

Tomatoes are also antioxidant-rich and contain plenty of vitamin C, which can prevent the cellular damage that leads to cancer. Watermelons, carrots and red peppers also contain these substances, but in lesser quantities.

There are some foods that should be avoided when following a cancer-fighting diet, or a healthy diet generally. Exclude all refined products such as biscuits, cakes, white breads and sugar-coated cereals. This will greatly help to reduce obesity, a contributory factor, and detox your body. Smoked, salt cured and pickled foods should also be avoided. Alcohol should be limited, but red wine contains powerful antioxidants called polyphenols that may protect against various types of cancer. However, alcohol can be toxic to the liver and nervous system, and some research has indicated that it may be a carcinogen. 'All things in moderation' should perhaps be your guide here.

The recipes in the Cancer Fighting Food section of this book (pages 58–97) are specifically designed to include a range of the best cancer-fighting foods, whether you have cancer and want to do all you can to beat it, or you are concerned that you may be at risk in the future. With delicious recipes such as Carrot & Ginger Soup, Citrus-grilled Plaice and Hot Herby Mushrooms, there is something here for everyone.

Combating High Blood Pressure

With our changing eating habits and lifestyle, high blood pressure is becoming more and more prevalent in the West. Medical experts attribute this in many cases to bad diet. In recent years we have been eating an increasing amount of processed convenience foods, relying on the freezer and microwave for our meals and eating take-away foods from fish and chips, burgers, and kebabs to pizza, Indian and Chinese food. This is coupled with an increase in sugary fizzy drinks, alcohol drinking, sweets, biscuits, cakes, crisps and instant snacks, designed to satisfy hunger pangs in a flash with no regard to the nutritional cost. Together with the majority of people not taking enough exercise – relying on the car rather than walking, sitting in front of the television or computer rather than playing sport – is it any wonder that for many our hearts are having a serious problem coping? The remedy is simple – we need to cut out the junk food, return to a well-cooked, nutritionally balanced diet and take regular exercise.

Our bodies rely totally on our hearts. It is the largest muscle in our body and controls the flow of blood. The heart pumps the five litres of blood that our body contains through the arteries into tiny capillaries which feed the body tissues before returning to the heart back through the veins (the circulatory system). This happens 75 times every single minute. An accurate indication of how healthy your heart is can be assessed by taking your blood pressure, essentially a measurement of how your heart is performing. There are two readings taken: the higher measurement records the blood flow at its peak while the heart is beating, and the lower measurement records the flow of blood when the heart is relaxing. An average normal reading is 120/80, but obviously there are always variations on this measurement.

As we grow older, the elasticity in the veins and arteries can reduce. Healthy veins and arteries expand and contract easily and the blood flows freely, but when, either due to poor health or age, they no longer work efficiently, high blood pressure occurs. Eating badly can thicken the arteries and have the same effect, making it harder for blood to get round the body, raising the pressure in the arteries and increasing the risk of problems. This can also happen on a temporary basis when you get upset, excited or frightened. The heart beats faster, pushing the blood more quickly round the body, and if the elasticity has decreased then a problem can occur such as stroke, heart attack or blood clots. However, there are steps that can be taken to either prevent or reduce this lack of elasticity, and that is by watching the diet.

As with all diseases, a healthy lifestyle is paramount to a healthy life and ensuring the body's organs work efficiently. If you have been diagnosed with high blood pressure, or your family have a history of heart problems, then it is essential that you look at your lifestyle and change it if necessary.

Many health experts believe that we eat too much salt, and this is a contributory factor in high blood pressure. The average body will get sufficient salt from a balanced diet but in the West on average we consume an extra 10–12 grams each day. Simply by reducing this amount, we are well on the way to addressing the problem. Try not putting salt in your food when it is being cooked, and instead use herbs or spices to flavour. You will be surprised how quickly your palate adjusts.

Preparing and cooking healthy dishes need not be a chore, and there are plenty of recipes that can be on the table in less than 30 minutes and will be tasty, more nutritious and satisfying than any take-away or fast food. You will also have the satisfaction of knowing that these dishes are doing you and your family's hearts good by either preventing or reducing high blood pressure.

To further reduce the risk of high blood pressure, there are a few simple rules to observe. Firstly it is vital to reduce the intake of all saturated fat, butter, lard, dripping, cream, whole milk, hard cheese and the fat from meats. Buy only lean meats and remove any fat before cooking. Remove the skin from poultry, as any fat in poultry is situated immediately under the skin. Use monounsaturated oils for cooking such as olive, soya or sunflower oil, but use sparingly and ban fried foods – especially deep fried foods – forever.

Include plenty of oily fish in your diet, such as mackerel, kippers, pilchards, sardines, salmon and trout. They are high in omega-3 fatty acids, an unsaturated fat that will help to eliminate the bad LDL cholesterol in your blood. It has been suggested that 115 g of oily fish 2–3 times a week dramatically reduces heart problems.

Most of us love pastries, cakes and biscuits, but unfortunately these are bad for us and need to be drastically cut back or eliminated. Limit the amount of sugary foods you eat – try keeping a slice of cake or a biscuit as a treat rather than the norm, and that way it will be more enjoyable and is one more step to a healthy lifestyle. It is not all bad news, though – there are plenty of delicious foods that can be eaten and will help maintain a healthy heart.

Increase your intake of high fibre foods, as these are not only extremely good for the body but they also help to keep the stomach feeling full and satiated, reducing the need for snacking on sugary sweets or salty snacks. Vegetables, fruit, pulses, rice and wholegrain cereals should all be eaten regularly. Soya beans and soya oil have proven to be very beneficial for the heart, and here in the West we tend to discount this very important food. Soya milk is also nutritionally excellent and if switched with whole milk would make a substantial difference to blood pressure levels.

For many there is a real bonus – it has been found that beer and wine drunk in moderation (and that is the key word – moderation!) – can play an important part in the diet. One glass of red wine or beer can help the cholesterol levels within the blood, thus improving blood pressure. Any benefits of this are negated by drinking to excess, though, so try not to over-indulge.

Lifestyle choices can also help to reduce high blood pressure. Try and spend more time relaxing and avoid stress wherever possible. Exercise more, starting slowly and gradually increasing how much you do. It is recommended that the heart needs to work faster for at least 20–30 minutes, three or four times a week but ideally each day for there to be an improvement. If you do not enjoy or are not capable of intensive exercise, a brisk walk every day will be just as beneficial. Finally, giving up smoking should be of paramount importance in your quest for a healthy heart.

To help your healthy lifestyle, the High Blood Pressure section of this book (pages 98–137) provides lots of delicious recipes that are easy to prepare and cook and ensure that flavour is not sacrificed for health. With tasty dishes from Turkey & Tomato Tagine to Chunky Halibut Casserole and Pad Thai, you will soon be on your way to a healthy heart.

Living with Food Allergies

More and more people seem to be suffering from all kinds of allergies, many of which are food and drink related. A food allergy is a reaction from the immune system to a food that the body mistakenly thinks is harmful. The immune system then creates specific antibodies to it, which means that the next time you eat that food the immune system releases massive amounts of chemicals, including histamine, in order to protect the body. These chemicals trigger a range of unpleasant symptoms, which can include nausea, breathing problems, rashes and skin irritation, headaches which can quickly become migraines, cramps and an upset stomach. The food involved can be any food or even a combination of foods, and if you suspect that you have an allergy or food intolerance it is important that you get this investigated so that you can eliminate it from your diet and improve your quality of life.

It is worth bearing in mind that there are varying degrees of allergies, and in some cases the problem is not an allergy but a food intolerance. Food intolerance is a general term that is applied to all reactions that occur after consuming food and drink and can be triggered not necessarily by the food, but by additives that have been artificially added – food colours, pesticides or fertilizers, preservatives and flavourings. Food allergies, on the other hand, are when the body's immune system has an abnormal and violent reaction to a particular food or additive. Food allergies can be triggered by any foods, such as fruits, vegetables and meats, but 90 per cent of reactions are caused by milk, eggs, peanuts, tree nuts (walnuts, cashews, etc.), fish, shellfish, soy and wheat. Reactions to these foods can be very extreme, and similar to how some people react to a bee or wasp sting. This is known as anaphylaxis and can be life threatening. People who are at risk of this should carry an antidote which can be administered immediately and carry a card stating their allergy reaction.

Recent research suggests that one in six people are affected by food allergies, so if you suspect you may be one of them you should see your doctor as soon as possible. If necessary they will refer you to a nutritionist. As well as skin testing, hair analysis and blood tests, a nutritionist may ask you to do an elimination trial in order to pinpoint the problem food groups. This involves eliminating certain foods over a period of time and then gradually re-introducing them to the diet. Once you have worked out which foods present a problem, you should be able to avoid them and thereby improve your well-being and quality of life dramatically.

If a member of your family has a food allergy, it does not necessarily mean you will also be at risk – a food that one person has a problem with can be completely harmless to another member of the same family. Recent research has also shown that food intolerance and allergies can be caused by an enzyme deficiency which can make a particular food difficult to digest.

A good example of this is lactose intolerance, which can affect very young babies. Some allergies can be outgrown, however, so a diagnosis of intolerance is not necessarily a life sentence.

If you are suffering from a food allergy, the first step is to look at your diet, but be sure to seek professional advice as described previously before trying a food elimination experiment. This will ensure that a balanced diet is maintained and a suitable substitute can be introduced if important foods are excluded. Some of the most common allergens are listed below.

Nuts, especially peanuts are one of the biggest culprits especially in young children. It is recommended that all nuts and products that contain nuts are not given to children under the age of five. Many convenience foods, from biscuits, cakes, desserts and ice cream to ready-meals and savoury products may contain nuts, or have been prepared on the same equipment as food containing nuts. Most are now clearly labelled, so checking the ingredient list is vital. Coconut, nutmeg and water chestnuts do not need to be avoided, however.

Cows' milk can also set up an allergic reaction – in this case the intestines cannot tolerate the lactose contained in the milk. Goats' milk protein is similar to that in cows' milk, so is not necessarily a safe alternative. Some people find they cannot digest full cream cows' milk but can tolerate in small amounts skimmed milk, so do not rule cows' milk out altogether until you have investigated this. An adverse reaction to cows' milk normally indicates that cheese, butter, yogurt and cream can also cause problems.

Egg whites can cause allergic reactions, and as eggs are in many products it is vital to read ingredient lists carefully. Toddlers normally seem to be the age group most likely to be affected by an allergy to eggs, but the good news is that they are likely to outgrow this particular intolerance.

Gluten intolerance seems to be increasing rapidly. The major grains that contain gluten are wheat, rye, oats and barley. These grains and their by-products must be strictly avoided by people with a gluten allergy, although wheat-allergic people need only avoid wheat. Rice flour, potato flour or cornflour are good substitutes for wheat flour in any recipe.

Berries such as strawberries and raspberries can cause a reaction, often swelling of the mouth. For some, kiwi fruits, citrus fruits and vegetables such as celery can also be a problem.

Soya beans can also cause a severe allergic reaction. Unfortunately they have become a major part of processed food products, so avoiding them can be difficult as well as possibly resulting in an unbalanced diet. They can be found in baked goods, canned tuna, cereals, crackers, infant formulas, sauces and soups, so always read the label.

Fish and shellfish are a common cause of allergic reactions in both adults and children. It is generally recommended that those who have had an allergic reaction to one species of fish avoid all fish, and the same goes for shellfish. Be aware that Worcestershire sauce often contains anchovies, as do Caesar salad dressings.

The Allergy Free section of this book (pages 138–177) gives recipes designed to help those suffering with the food allergies or intolerances discussed here. It is important to note, however, that whilst we have tried to eliminate or substitute the most obvious causes of allergic reactions, there may still be ingredients that disagree with certain people. Please therefore read the recipe very carefully before cooking, and leave out anything that you think might cause a problem. But, with tasty dishes such as Coconut-baked Courgettes and Chilli Roast Chicken, there should be something for everyone.

Living with Wheat & Gluten Intolerances

Many medical conditions can be improved and made more tolerable and easier to live with by diet. This is especially true with wheat and gluten intolerance. By following a wheat and gluten-free diet it is possible to live a normal life with very little pain or discomfort. An intolerance to gluten, also known as coeliac disease, is when the small intestines cannot digest gluten, a protein found in wheat, rye, oats, barley and their products. The gluten can damage the intestinal lining, which has a knock-on effect as it can result in the sufferer not being able to properly absorb any food they eat.

Without an early diagnosis this can result, in the most drastic cases, in malnutrition, anaemia, osteoporosis and other complaints. Even in its mildest form it can cause much pain, discomfort and stomach upsets. It is not a contagious disease but can run in families.

There is a difference between coeliac disease and wheat intolerance. Wheat intolerance is an allergy just to wheat and all its products, and has a variety of symptoms. Sneezing, itching, rashes, watery eyes, runny nose, hay fever, coughing, headaches, breathing difficulties, digestive

problems and swollen painful limbs can all be experienced.

Wheat intolerance can be diagnosed by a simple blood or skin test, whereas coeliac disease needs an intestinal biopsy, often under a mild sedation. Coeliac disease tends to affect young children and it is not uncommon to outgrow the problem. It is not detectable when the child is a very young baby and usually only becomes apparent after weaning, once other foods are introduced to the diet. Symptoms can include violent stomach cramps and pains as well as vomiting and diarrhoea. If your child is slow to put on weight, cries often, is anaemic and is generally miserable and unwell, it might well be worth experimenting with their diet, with the approval of your doctor. A great improvement can be seen simply by excluding wheat from the diet.

Coeliac disease is not only confined to children. According to The Coeliac Society, the majority of adult sufferers are diagnosed between the ages of 35–40, and this is on the increase. An adult's symptoms can be more serious, including weight loss, vomiting, diarrhoea or (conversely) constipation, anaemia (which leads to tiredness and lethargy), flatulence, mouth ulcers, painful joints, depression and, in some cases, infertility.

Wheat as well as oats, rye and barley need to be eliminated from the diet in order to alleviate this intolerance. This can be very hard, as a huge number of foods have 'hidden' sources of gluten. The most obvious things to avoid are bread, biscuits, cakes, pastries, many breakfast cereals, pasta, pizza, pies and some meat products (cereal-based ingredients containing wheat can be used as a bulk filler). When buying convenience foods, it is important that the ingredient list is read very carefully. Also bear in mind that when first embarking on this kind of diet, it will be necessary to check the larder and freezer so that any foods containing the offending gluten or wheat can be removed.

Although this rules out many foods, it is not all doom and gloom. There is a growing range of wheat and gluten free products available from most large supermarkets, health food shops and over the internet, including bread, pasta, biscuits, flour and cakes. These foods have had the gluten removed and substitutes are added from other sources. Substitutes such as rice, tapioca, buckwheat and cornflour can also be used instead. The recipes in this book have been specifically designed to be wheat and gluten free, but you can use many of these substitutes when adapting your own favourite recipes. Some of the most common substitutes are detailed below.

Sugar beet fibre is the dietary fibre from the sugar beet left after the sugar has been extracted. It contains a natural balance of insoluble and soluble fibre, with the soluble fibre being nutritionally beneficial.

Rice is one of the oldest grains in the world and is grown extensively. There are many varieties and it is highly suitable for those with food intolerances as it is easily digested.

Potato starch is produced by a potato that is first cleaned and then the starch and the juices are extracted separately to produce a milky liquid. This is purified and dried, forming starch granules.

Carob beans are the pods from the carob tree originating in the Mediterranean and parts of Asia. The pods contain a high degree of natural sugars and fibre, have a low sugar content and have the added advantage of a rich vitamin and mineral content.

Xanthan gum is produced by the fermentation of sugar with friendly bacteria. It is often mixed with corn syrup.

Buckwheat is no relation to wheat and is a member of the rhubarb family. The flowers are harvested after ripening and the buckwheat or seeds are removed and can be milled to provide a fine flour, or simply boiled.

Maize or corn contains no wheat or gluten and can be found in a variety of products, from oil and flour to breakfast cereals.

Tapioca comes from the cassava tree and is from the inner part of the root. Grown in Central America, Brazil and Africa it forms an integral part of the diet of these people.

Gram or channa dal comes from the chick pea family. It can be milled into a fine yellow flour, rich in natural goodness and a gluten-free source of protein and fibre.

Recent research has also shown that some sufferers can eat oats as well, but it is strongly recommended that you talk to your doctor about this first.

If following a gluten-free diet, it may be necessary to supplement it as certain vitamins and minerals may be lacking, especially the B vitamins, magnesium, phosphorous and selenium. As wheat is a complex carbohydrate it is important that sufficient fibre is eaten in order to maintain a balanced diet.

The recipes in the Wheat and Gluten Free section (pages 178–217) have been designed to allow those intolerant of gluten and wheat to eat delicious meals that add to their quality of life. With dishes such as Crown Roast of Lamb and Almond Macaroons, you will be able to experience all the joys of eating without worrying about your health.

Some information for this introduction was taken from www.dovesfarm.co.uk

Living a Dairy–free Life

For some, the eating of any dairy products causes much misery and discomfort. For one reason or another people can be allergic to some or all dairy foods, which can include milk, yogurt, cream, butter and most cheeses. In some cases babies are born with an intolerance to lactose (present in cows' milk), and unless diagnosed early this can have a very disruptive effect. Often as the baby becomes a toddler they outgrow this intolerance. However, there are those who either do not or, for some reason, develop an intolerance to dairy products at a later date. In many cases there seems to be no reason for this, although some food experts feel that this reaction is due to intensive methods of farming and the way that animals are reared.

It is not only those who suffer an allergic reaction when eating dairy products who follow a dairy-free diet. For some, especially those following a low-fat diet, it makes perfect sense. Dairy products are high in saturated fats, meaning high cholesterol and calorie levels. So for those following a healthy heart or weight loss program, or those who are strict vegetarians or vegans, a dairy-free diet can be very beneficial.

For those who suffer a severe reaction when eating dairy products, the most probable reason is to do with the digestive system. Those who are lactose-intolerant do not produce the necessary enzymes needed to break down the sugar (called lactose) found in dairy products and the body cannot therefore absorb it. This can cause some distressing symptoms, including nausea, cramps, bloating, gas and an upset stomach. There is currently no cure for an intolerance to lactose, but the condition can be controlled by avoiding dairy products. The recipes in this book will help you to do this.

Many respected scientists and food experts feel that these problems, which have undoubtedly increased over the last fifty years, can be traced back to intensive farming methods. After the Second World War, the government

and its products are pasteurised or not when abroad.

If you are following a dairy-free diet it is important that the calcium and vitamins that we derive from milk are replaced wuth other foods that contain them. Tofu, fish, especially salmon, all green leafy vegetables, nuts, sesame seeds and fruits such as dates are all good sources of calcium.

These days there are many substitutes for dairy products. Soya, rice, oat, almond, sunflower and coconut milks and their products make excellent substitutes and are available in most health food shops. Butter can be replaced with spreads made from vegetable or olive oils, and dairy-free butter is also available from larger supermarkets. Dairy-free cheeses are slightly more hit-and-miss, but again are available from supermarkets, as are soya creams, yogurts and ice creams.

The last section of this book, Dairy Free (pages 218–25), provides recipes that do not include any dairy products. There is a good selection of recipes to inspire you to cook healthy, nutritious meals suitable for all the family. From Aromatic Duck Burgers on Potato Pancakes to a Coconut Fish Curry and Braised Chicken in Beer, there is something for everyone here, whether they are following a dairy-free diet or not.

instructed farmers to farm intensively in order that the country could not only feed its population but also have more than was needed. The excess could then be exported and less produce would need to be imported, thus helping the balance of payments. This intensive farming meant that fields where cattle herds grazed were treated with pesticides and the animal themselves were injected with growth hormones. This ensured that the animals came to maturity earlier and the milk yield was vastly increased. Animals were also regularly injected against disease.

Slowly, as more and more problems have appeared within the food chain, a backlash has occurred. There is a growing demand for animals to be treated more humanely and reared organically. A few farmers had continued or have returned to this method of traditional farming, and now the movement for organic farming – where the cattle are not treated with hormones and do not graze on land that has been treated with pesticides – is steadily increasing. In theory at least, this ensures that neither the meat nor the milk and all the products that are made from the milk are contaminated. It has long been thought that these artificial hormones and pesticides can seriously affect the digestive system and set up allergies or a dairy intolerance.

In the United Kingdom, most milk and milk products are treated before being consumed, normally by pasteurisation. This is a heat treatment that destroys any toxins that may be present in the milk or its products, such as yogurt, cheese, butter and cream. Unfortunately it also destroys the vitamins – especially vitamin D – contained in the milk. So the result is that these vitamins are artificially replaced. Some other countries still regularly use unpasteurised or 'raw' milk, so if there is any tendency to digestive or stomach problems it is a good idea to check whether the milk

High Fibre

Fibre is essential for a healthy lifestyle and diets that are low in fibre lead to constipation and bowel disorders. It is recommended that we eat 24 g of fibre per day to retain a healthy lifestyle. The following recipes are designed to help you get as much fibre into your diet as possible in delicious and interesting ways.

Cream of Pumpkin Soup

INGREDIENTS

Serves 4

900 g/2 lb pumpkin flesh
  (after peeling and discarding
  the seeds)
4 tbsp olive oil
1 large onion, peeled
1 leek, trimmed
1 carrot, peeled
2 celery sticks
4 garlic cloves, peeled and crushed
1.7 litres/3 pints water
salt and freshly ground black pepper
$\frac{1}{4}$ tsp freshly grated nutmeg
150 ml/$\frac{1}{4}$ pint single cream
$\frac{1}{4}$ tsp cayenne pepper

1 Cut the skinned and deseeded pumpkin flesh into 2.5 cm/1 inch cubes. Heat the olive oil in a large saucepan and cook the pumpkin for 2–3 minutes, coating it completely with oil. Chop the onion and leek finely and cut the carrot and celery into small cubes.

2 Add the vegetables to the saucepan with the garlic and cook, stirring for 5 minutes, or until they have begun to soften. Cover the vegetables with the water and bring to the boil. Season with plenty of salt and pepper and the nutmeg, then cover and simmer for 15–20 minutes, or until all of the vegetables are tender.

3 When the vegetables are tender, remove from the heat, cool slightly then pour into a food processor or blender. Liquidise to form a smooth purée then pass through a sieve into a clean saucepan.

4 Adjust the seasoning to taste and add all but 2 tablespoons of the cream and enough water to obtain the correct consistency. Bring the soup to boiling point, add the cayenne pepper and serve immediately swirled with cream.

Nutritional details per 100 g   energy 62 kcals/260 kj · protein 2 g · carbohydrate 8 g · fat 3 g · fibre 1.3 g · sugar 2.5 g · sodium 0.1 g

◖ cows' milk-free   ✓ egg-free   ✓ gluten-free   ✓ wheat-free   ✓ nut-free   ✓ vegetarian   ◖ vegan   ✓ seafood-free

Aduki Bean & Rice Burgers

INGREDIENTS

Serves 4

2½ tbsp sunflower oil
1 medium onion, peeled and
  very finely chopped
1 garlic clove, peeled and crushed
1 tsp curry paste
225 g/8 oz basmati rice
400 g can aduki beans,
  drained and rinsed
225 ml/8 fl oz vegetable stock
125 g/4 oz firm tofu, crumbled
1 tsp garam masala
2 tbsp freshly chopped coriander
salt and freshly ground
  black pepper

For the carrot raita:

2 large carrots, peeled and grated
½ cucumber, cut into tiny cubes
150 ml/¼ pint Greek yogurt

To serve:

wholemeal baps
tomato slices
lettuce leaves

1 Heat 1 tablespoon of the oil in a saucepan and gently cook the onion for 10 minutes until soft. Add the garlic and curry paste and cook for a few more seconds. Stir in the rice and beans.

2 Pour in the stock, bring to the boil and simmer for 12 minutes, or until all the stock has been absorbed – do not lift the lid for the first 10 minutes of cooking. Reserve.

3 Lightly mash the tofu. Add to the rice mixture with the garam masala, coriander, salt and pepper. Mix.

4 Divide the mixture into eight and shape into burgers. Chill in the refrigerator for 30 minutes.

5 Meanwhile, make the raita. Mix together the carrots, cucumber and Greek yogurt. Spoon into a small bowl and chill in the refrigerator until ready to serve.

6 Heat the remaining oil in a large frying pan. Fry the burgers, in batches if necessary, for 4–5 minutes on each side, or until lightly browned. Serve in the baps with tomato slices and lettuce. Accompany with the raita.

Nutritional details per 100 g   energy 104 kcals/436 kj · protein 5 g · carbohydrate 15 g · fat 3 g · fibre 2.2 g · sugar 2.7 g · sodium 0.2 g

cows' milk-free   ✓ egg-free   gluten-free   wheat-free   ✓ nut-free   ✓ vegetarian   vegan   ✓ seafood-free

3

4

5

Braised Chicken with Aubergine

INGREDIENTS

Serves 6

3 tbsp vegetable oil

12 chicken thighs

2 large aubergines, trimmed
  and cubed

4 garlic cloves, peeled and crushed

2 tsp freshly grated root ginger

900 ml/1½ pints vegetable stock

2 tbsp light soy sauce

2 tbsp Chinese preserved black beans

6 spring onions, trimmed and
  thinly sliced diagonally

1 tbsp cornflour

1 tbsp sesame oil

spring onion tassels, to garnish

freshly cooked noodles or rice,
  to serve

1 Heat a wok or large frying pan, add the oil and when hot, add the chicken thighs and cook over a medium high heat for 5 minutes, or until browned all over. Transfer to a large plate and keep warm.

2 Add the aubergine to the wok and cook over a high heat for 5 minutes or until browned, turning occasionally. Add the garlic and ginger and stir-fry for 1 minute.

3 Return the chicken to the wok, pour in the stock and add the soy sauce and black beans. Bring to the boil, then simmer for 20 minutes, or until the chicken is tender. Add the spring onions after 10 minutes.

4 Blend the cornflour with 2 tablespoons of water. Stir into the wok and simmer until the sauce has thickened. Stir in the sesame oil, heat for 30 seconds, then remove from the heat. Garnish with spring onion tassels and serve immediately with noodles or rice.

Nutritional details per 100 g energy 80 kcals/337 kj · protein 7 g · carbohydrate 7 g · fat 3 g · fibre 1 g · sugar 0.2 g · sodium 0.2 g

✓ cows' milk-free   ✓ egg-free   ◖ gluten-free   ◖ wheat-free   ✓ nut-free   ◖ vegetarian   ◖ vegan   ✓ seafood-free

Broad Bean & Artichoke Risotto

INGREDIENTS

Serves 4

275 g/10 oz frozen broad beans

400 g can artichoke hearts, drained

1 tbsp sunflower oil

150 ml/¼ pint dry white wine

900 ml/1½ pints vegetable stock

25 g/1 oz butter

1 onion, peeled and finely chopped

200 g/7 oz Arborio rice

finely grated rind and juice of 1 lemon

50 g/2 oz Parmesan cheese, grated

salt and freshly ground black pepper

freshly grated Parmesan cheese,
   to serve

1 Cook the beans in a saucepan of lightly salted boiling water for 4–5 minutes, or until just tender. Drain and plunge into cold water. Peel off the tough outer skins, if liked. Pat the artichokes dry on absorbent kitchen paper and cut each in half lengthways through the stem end. Cut each half into three wedges.

2 Heat the oil in a large saucepan and cook the artichokes for 4–5 minutes, turning occasionally, until they are lightly browned. Remove and reserve. Bring the wine and stock to the boil in a separate frying pan. Keep them barely simmering while making the risotto.

3 Melt the butter in a large frying pan, add the onion and cook for 5 minutes until beginning to soften. Add the rice and cook for 1 minute, stirring. Pour in a ladleful of the hot wine and stock and simmer gently, stirring, until the stock is absorbed. Continue to add the stock in this way for 20–25 minutes, until the rice is just tender; the risotto should look creamy and soft.

4 Add the broad beans, artichokes, and lemon rind and juice. Gently mix in, cover and leave to warm through for 1–2 minutes. Stir in the Parmesan cheese and season to taste with salt and pepper. Serve sprinkled with extra Parmesan cheese.

Nutritional details per 100 g energy 99 kcals/412 kj · protein 5 g · carbohydrate 11 g · fat 4 g · fibre 1.4 g · sugar 0.9 g · sodium 0.4 g

 cows' milk-free   ✓ egg-free   gluten-free   wheat-free   ✓ nut-free   ✓ vegetarian   vegan   ✓ seafood-free

Brown Rice & Lentil Salad with Duck

INGREDIENTS

Serves 6

225 g/8 oz Puy lentils, rinsed

4 tbsp olive oil

1 medium onion, peeled and
  finely chopped

200 g/7 oz long-grain brown rice

½ tsp dried thyme

450 ml/¾ pint chicken stock

salt and freshly ground black pepper

350 g/12 oz shiitake or portabella
  mushrooms, trimmed and sliced

375 g/13 oz cooked Chinese-style
  spicy duck or roasted duck,
  sliced into chunks

2 garlic cloves, peeled and
  finely chopped

125 g/4 oz cooked smoked ham, diced

2 small courgettes, trimmed,
  diced and blanched

6 spring onions, trimmed and
  thinly sliced

2 tbsp freshly chopped parsley

2 tbsp walnut halves,
  toasted and chopped

1 Bring a large saucepan of water to the boil, sprinkle in the lentils, return to the boil, then simmer over a low heat for 30 minutes, or until tender; do not overcook. Drain and rinse under cold running water, then drain again and reserve.

2 Heat 2 tablespoons of the oil in a saucepan. Add the onion and cook for 2 minutes until it begins to soften. Stir in the rice with the thyme and stock. Season to taste with salt and pepper and bring to the boil. Cover and simmer for 40 minutes, or until tender and the liquid is absorbed.

3 Heat the remaining oil in a large frying pan and add the mushrooms. Cook for 5 minutes until golden. Stir in the duck and garlic and cook for 2–3 minutes to heat through. Season well.

4 To make the dressing, whisk 2 tablespoons of red or white wine vinegar, 1 tablespoon of balsamic vinegar, 1 teaspoon of Dijon mustard and 1 teaspoon of clear honey in a large serving bowl, then gradually whisk in 75ml/3fl oz of extra-virgin olive oil and 2 or 3 tablespoons of walnut oil. Add the lentils and the rice, then stir lightly together. Gently stir in the ham, blanched courgettes, spring onions and parsley. Season to taste and sprinkle with the walnuts. Serve topped with the duck and mushrooms.

Nutritional details per 100 g energy 117 kcals/724 kj · protein 10 g · carbohydrate 9 g · fat 12 g · fibre 1 g · sugar 1.2 g · sodium 0.3 g

✓ cows' milk-free   ✓ egg-free   gluten-free   wheat-free   nut-free   vegetarian   vegan   ✓ seafood-free

Cheese & Onion Oat Pie

INGREDIENTS

Serves 4

1 tbsp sunflower oil, plus 1 tsp
25 g/1 oz butter
2 medium onions, peeled and sliced
1 garlic clove, peeled and crushed
150 g/5 oz porridge oats
125 g/4 oz mature Cheddar
  cheese, grated
2 medium eggs, lightly beaten
2 tbsp freshly chopped parsley
salt and freshly ground black pepper
275 g/10 oz baking potato, peeled

1   Preheat the oven to 180°C/350°F/Gas Mark 4. Heat the oil and half the butter in a saucepan until melted. Add the onions and garlic and gently cook for 10 minutes, or until soft. Remove from the heat and tip into a large bowl.

2   Spread the oats out onto a baking sheet and toast in the hot oven for 12 minutes. Leave to cool, then add to the onions with the cheese, eggs and parsley. Season to taste with salt and pepper and mix well.

3   Line the base of a 20.5 cm/8 inch round sandwich tin with greaseproof paper and oil well. Thinly slice the potato and arrange the slices on the base, overlapping them slightly.

4   Spoon the cheese and oat mixture on top of the potato, spreading evenly with the back of a spoon. Cover with tinfoil and bake for 30 minutes.

5   Invert the pie onto a baking sheet so that the potatoes are on top. Carefully remove the tin and lining paper.

6   Preheat the grill to medium. Melt the remaining butter and carefully brush over the potato topping. Cook under the preheated grill for 5–6 minutes until the potatoes are lightly browned. Cut into wedges and serve.

Nutritional details per 100 g   energy 187 kcals/781 kj · protein 8 g · carbohydrate 18 g · fat 10 g · fibre 1 g · sugar 2 g · sodium 0.2 g

 cows' milk-free   egg-free   gluten-free   ✓ wheat-free   ✓ nut-free   ✓ vegetarian   vegan   ✓ seafood-free

2

3

6

Creamy Puy Lentils

INGREDIENTS

Serves 4

225 g/8 oz puy lentils
1 tbsp olive oil
1 garlic clove, peeled and
  finely chopped
zest and juice of 1 lemon
1 tsp wholegrain mustard
1 tbsp freshly chopped tarragon
3 tbsp half-fat crème fraîche
salt and freshly ground black pepper
2 small tomatoes, deseeded
  and chopped
50 g/2 oz pitted black olives
1 tbsp freshly chopped parsley

To garnish:
sprigs of fresh tarragon
lemon wedges

1 Put the lentils into a saucepan with plenty of cold water and bring to the boil.

2 Boil rapidly for 10 minutes, reduce the heat and simmer gently for a further 20 minutes until just tender. Drain well.

3 Meanwhile, prepare the dressing. Heat the oil in a frying pan over a medium heat.

4 Add the garlic and cook for about a minute until just beginning to brown. Add the lemon zest and juice.

5 Add the mustard and cook for a further 30 seconds.

6 Add the tarragon and crème fraîche and season to taste with salt and pepper.

7 Simmer and add the drained lentils, tomatoes and olives.

8 Transfer to a serving dish and sprinkle the chopped parsley on top.

9 Garnish the lentils with the tarragon sprigs and the lemon wedges and serve immediately.

Nutritional details per 100 g   energy 84 kcals/353 kj · protein 4 g · carbohydrate 10 g · fat 4 g · fibre 2.2 g · sugar 1 g · sodium 0.3 g

⬤ cows' milk-free   ✓ egg-free   ⬤ gluten-free   ⬤ wheat-free   ✓ nut-free   ✓ vegetarian   ⬤ vegan   ✓ seafood-free

1

4

7

Mixed Grain Pilaf

INGREDIENTS

Serves 4

2 tbsp olive oil

1 garlic clove, peeled and crushed

½ tsp ground turmeric

125 g/4 oz mixed long-grain
  and wild rice

50 g/2 oz red lentils

300 ml/½ pint vegetable stock

200 g can chopped tomatoes

5 cm/2 inch piece cinnamon stick

salt and freshly ground black pepper

400 g can mixed beans, drained
  and rinsed

15 g/½ oz butter

1 bunch spring onions, trimmed
  and finely sliced

3 medium eggs

4 tbsp freshly chopped herbs,
  such as parsley and chervil

sprigs of fresh dill, to garnish

1 Heat 1 tablespoon of the oil in a saucepan. Add the garlic and turmeric and cook for a few seconds. Stir in the rice and lentils.

2 Add the stock, tomatoes and cinnamon. Season to taste with salt and pepper. Stir once and bring to the boil. Lower the heat, cover and simmer for 20 minutes, until most of the stock is absorbed and the rice and lentils are tender.

3 Stir in the beans, replace the lid and leave to stand for 2–3 minutes to allow the beans to heat through.

4 While the rice is cooking, heat the remaining oil and butter in a frying pan. Add the spring onions and cook for 4–5 minutes, until soft. Lightly beat the eggs with 2 tablespoons of the herbs, then season with salt and pepper.

5 Pour the egg mixture over the spring onions. Stir gently with a spatula over a low heat, drawing the mixture from the sides to the centre as the omelette sets. When almost set, stop stirring and cook for about 30 seconds until golden underneath.

6 Remove the omelette from the pan, roll up and slice into thin strips. Fluff the rice up with a fork and remove the cinnamon stick. Spoon onto serving plates, top with strips of omelette and the remaining chopped herbs. Garnish with sprigs of dill and serve.

Nutritional details per 100 g energy 98 kcals/412 kj · protein 5 g · carbohydrate 10 g · fat 4 g · fibre 2.5 g · sugar 2.3 g · sodium 0.3 g

◖ cows' milk-free ◖ egg-free ◖ gluten-free ◖ wheat-free ✓ nut-free ✓ vegetarian ◖ vegan ✓ seafood-free

Pork in Peanut Sauce

INGREDIENTS

Serves 4

450 g/1 lb pork fillet
2 tbsp light soy sauce
1 tbsp vinegar
1 tsp sugar
1 tsp Chinese five-spice powder
2–4 garlic cloves, peeled and crushed
2 tbsp groundnut oil
1 large onion, peeled and finely sliced
125 g/4 oz carrots, peeled and
  cut into matchsticks
2 celery sticks, trimmed and sliced
125 g/4 oz French beans, trimmed
  and halved
3 tbsp smooth peanut butter
1 tbsp freshly chopped
  flat-leaf parsley

To serve:

freshly cooked basmati and wild rice
green salad

1 Remove any fat or sinew from the pork fillet, cut into thin strips and reserve. Blend the soy sauce, vinegar, sugar, Chinese five-spice powder and garlic in a bowl and add the pork. Cover and leave to marinate in the refrigerator for at least 30 minutes.

2 Drain the pork, reserving any marinade. Heat the wok, then add the oil and, when hot, stir-fry the pork for 3–4 minutes, or until sealed.

3 Add the onion, carrots, celery and beans to the wok and stir-fry for 4–5 minutes, or until the meat is tender and the vegetables are softened.

4 Blend the reserved marinade, the peanut butter and 2 tablespoons of hot water together. When smooth, stir into the wok and cook for several minutes more until the sauce is thick and the pork is piping hot. Sprinkle with the chopped parsley and serve immediately with the basmati and wild rice and a green salad.

Nutritional details per 100 g   energy 117 kcals/490 kj · protein 11 g · carbohydrate 8 g · fat 5 g · fibre 1 g · sugar 1.9 g · sodium 0.2 g

✓ cows' milk-free   ✓ egg-free   gluten-free   wheat-free   nut-free   vegetarian   vegan   ✓ seafood-free

1

3

4

Potato Skins

INGREDIENTS

Serves 4

4 large baking potatoes
2 tbsp olive oil
2 tsp paprika
125 g/4 oz pancetta, roughly chopped
6 tbsp double cream
125 g/4 oz Gorgonzola cheese
1 tbsp freshly chopped parsley

To serve:

mayonnaise
sweet chilli dipping sauce

1 Preheat the oven to 200°C/400°F/Gas Mark 6. Scrub the potatoes, then prick a few times with a fork or skewer and place directly onto the top shelf of the oven. Bake in the preheated oven for at least 1 hour, or until tender. The potatoes are cooked when they yield gently to the pressure of your hand.

2 Set the potatoes aside until cool enough to handle, then cut in half and scoop the flesh into a bowl and reserve. Preheat the grill and line the grill rack with tinfoil.

3 Mix together the oil and the paprika and use half to brush the outside of the potato skins. Place on the grill rack under the preheated hot grill and cook for 5 minutes, or until crisp, turning as necessary.

4 Heat the remaining paprika-flavoured oil and gently fry the pancetta until crisp. Add to the potato flesh along with the cream, Gorgonzola cheese and parsley. Halve the potato skins and fill with the Gorgonzola filling. Return to the oven for a further 15 minutes to heat through. Sprinkle with a little more paprika and serve immediately with mayonnaise, sweet chilli sauce and a green salad.

Nutritional details per 100 g energy 222 kcals/927 kj · protein 6 g · carbohydrate 20 g · fat 8 g · fibre 1.7 g · sugar 1.2 g · sodium 0.3 g

cows' milk-free · egg-free · gluten-free · wheat-free · ✓ nut-free · vegetarian · vegan · ✓ seafood-free

2

3

4

Red Lentil Kedgeree with Avocado & Tomatoes

INGREDIENTS

Serves 4

150 g/5 oz basmati rice

150 g/5 oz red lentils

15 g/½ oz butter

1 tbsp sunflower oil

1 medium onion, peeled and chopped

1 tsp ground cumin

4 cardamom pods, bruised

1 bay leaf

450 ml/¾ pint vegetable stock

1 ripe avocado, peeled, stoned
  and diced

1 tbsp lemon juice

4 plum tomatoes, peeled
  and diced

2 tbsp freshly chopped coriander

salt and freshly ground black pepper

lemon or lime slices, to garnish

1 Put the rice and lentils in a sieve and rinse under cold running water. Tip into a bowl, then pour over enough cold water to cover and leave to soak for 10 minutes.

2 Heat the butter and oil in a saucepan. Add the sliced onion and cook gently, stirring occasionally, for 10 minutes until softened. Stir in the cumin, cardamon pods and bay leaf and cook for a further minute, stirring all the time.

3 Drain the rice and lentils, rinse again and add to the onions in the saucepan. Stir in the vegetable stock and bring to the boil. Reduce the heat, cover the saucepan and simmer for about 15 minutes, or until the rice and lentils are tender.

4 Place the diced avocado in a bowl and toss with the lemon juice. Stir in the tomatoes and chopped coriander. Season to taste with salt and pepper.

5 Fluff up the rice with a fork, spoon into a warmed serving dish and spoon the avocado mixture on top. Garnish with lemon or lime slices and serve.

Nutritional details per 100 g   energy 138 kcals/575 kj · protein 3 g · carbohydrate 13 g · fat 5 g · fibre 1.5 g · sugar 1.6 g · sodium 0.3 g

◖ cows' milk-free   ✓ egg-free   ◖ gluten-free   ◖ wheat-free   ✓ nut-free   ✓ vegetarian   ◖ vegan   ✓ seafood-free

2

4

5

Roast Butternut Squash Risotto

INGREDIENTS

Serves 4

1 medium butternut squash
2 tbsp olive oil
1 garlic bulb, cloves separated,
  but unpeeled
15 g/½ oz unsalted butter
275 g/10 oz Arborio rice
large pinch of saffron strands
150 ml/¼ pint dry white wine
1 litre/1¾ pints vegetable stock
1 tbsp freshly chopped parsley
1 tbsp freshly chopped oregano
50 g/2 oz Parmesan cheese,
  finely grated
salt and freshly ground black pepper
sprigs of fresh oregano, to garnish
extra Parmesan cheese, to serve

1 Preheat the oven to 190°C/375°F/Gas Mark 5. Cut the squash in half, peel, then scoop out the seeds and discard. Cut the flesh into 2 cm/ ¾ inch cubes.

2 Pour the oil into a large roasting tin and heat in the preheated oven for 5 minutes. Add the butternut squash and garlic cloves. Turn in the oil to coat, then roast in the oven for about 25–30 minutes, or until golden brown and very tender, turning the vegetables halfway through cooking time.

3 Melt the butter in a large saucepan. Add the rice and stir over a high heat for a few seconds. Add the saffron and the wine and bubble fiercely until almost totally reduced, stirring frequently. At the same time heat the stock in a separate saucepan and keep at a steady simmer.

4 Reduce the heat under the rice to low. Add a ladleful of stock to the saucepan and simmer, stirring, until absorbed. Continue adding the stock in this way until the rice is tender. This will take about 20 minutes and it may not be necessary to add all the stock.

5 Turn off the heat, stir in the herbs, Parmesan cheese and seasoning. Cover and leave to stand for 2–3 minutes. Quickly remove the skins from the roasted garlic. Add to the risotto with the butternut squash and mix gently. Garnish with sprigs of oregano and serve immediately with Parmesan cheese.

Nutritional details per 100 g energy 88 kcals/368 kj · protein 3 g · carbohydrate 11 g · fat 4 g · fibre 0.8 g · sugar 0.1 g · sodium 0.2 g

(cows' milk-free   ✓ egg-free   (gluten-free   (wheat-free   ✓ nut-free   ✓ vegetarian   (vegan   ✓ seafood-free

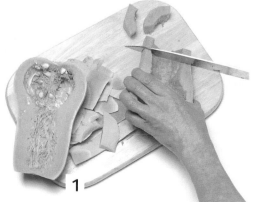

1

2

4

Smoked Salmon with Broad Beans & Rice

INGREDIENTS

Serves 4

2 tbsp sunflower oil

25 g/1 oz unsalted butter

1 onion, peeled and chopped

2 garlic cloves, peeled
  and chopped

175 g/6 oz asparagus tips, halved

75 g/3 oz frozen broad beans

150 ml/¼ pint dry white wine

125 g/4 oz sun-dried tomatoes,
  drained and sliced

125 g/4 oz baby spinach
  leaves, washed

450 g/1 lb cooked long-grain rice

3 tbsp crème fraîche

225 g/8 oz smoked salmon,
  cut into strips

75 g/3 oz freshly grated
  Parmesan cheese

salt and freshly ground
  black pepper

1 Heat a large wok, then add the oil and butter and, when melted, stir-fry the onion for 3 minutes until almost softened. Add the garlic and asparagus tips and stir-fry for 3 minutes. Add the broad beans and wine and bring to the boil, then simmer, stirring occasionally, until the wine is reduced slightly.

2 Add the sun-dried tomatoes and bring back to the boil, then simmer for 2 minutes. Stir in the baby spinach leaves and cooked rice and return to the boil. Stir-fry for 2 minutes, or until the spinach is wilted and the rice is heated through thoroughly.

3 Stir in the crème fraîche, smoked salmon strips and Parmesan cheese. Stir well and cook, stirring frequently, until piping hot. Season to taste with salt and pepper. Serve immediately.

Nutritional details per 100 g   energy 133 kcals/554 kj · protein 8 g · carbohydrate 10 g · fat 5 g · fibre 1 g · sugar 0.9 g · sodium 0.4 g

◖ cows' milk-free   ✓ egg-free   ◖ gluten-free   ✓ wheat-free   ✓ nut-free   ◖ vegetarian   ◖ vegan   ◖ seafood-free

Oaty Fruit Puddings

INGREDIENTS

Serves 4

125 g/4 oz rolled oats
50 g/2 oz butter, melted
2 tbsp chopped almonds
1 tbsp clear honey
pinch of ground cinnamon
2 pears, peeled, cored and
  finely chopped
1 tbsp marmalade
orange zest, to decorate
custard, to serve

1 Preheat the oven to 200°C/400°F/Gas Mark 6.

2 Lightly oil and line the bases of four individual pudding bowls or muffin tins with a small circle of greaseproof paper.

3 Mix together the oats, butter, nuts, honey and cinnamon in a small bowl.

4 Using a spoon, spread two thirds of the oaty mixture over the base and around the sides of the pudding bowls or muffin tins.

5 Toss together the pears and marmalade and spoon into the oaty cases.

6 Scatter over the remaining oaty mixture to cover the pears and marmalade.

7 Bake in the preheated oven for 15–20 minutes, until cooked and the tops of the puddings are golden and crisp.

8 Leave for 5 minutes before removing the pudding bowls or the muffin tins. Decorate with orange zest and serve hot with custard.

Nutritional details per 100 g   energy 138 kcals/581 kj · protein 5 g · carbohydrate 23 g · fat 3 g · fibre 1.2 g · sugar 12 g · sodium trace

◖ cows' milk-free   ◖ egg-free   ◖ gluten-free   ✓ wheat-free   ✓ nut-free   ◕ vegetarian   ◖ vegan   ◕ seafood-free

2   4   5

Cancer Fighting Food

Current research suggests that there is a link between cancer and the food that we eat. A poor diet may increase our chances of developing cancer. Conversely, certain foods have been singled out as being particularly good at fighting the disease. The following sumptuous recipes include as many of these 'superfoods' as possible.

Carrot & Ginger Soup

INGREDIENTS

Serves 4

4 slices of bread, crusts removed
1 tsp yeast extract
2 tsp olive oil
1 onion, peeled and chopped
1 garlic clove, peeled
  and crushed
½ tsp ground ginger
450 g/1 lb carrots, peeled
  and chopped
1 litre/1¾ pint vegetable stock
2.5 cm/1 inch piece of root ginger,
  peeled and finely grated
salt and freshly ground
  black pepper
1 tbsp lemon juice

To garnish:

chives
lemon zest

1 Preheat the oven to 180°C/350°F/Gas Mark 4. Roughly chop the bread. Dissolve the yeast extract in 2 tablespoons of warm water and mix with the bread.

2 Spread the bread cubes over a lightly oiled baking tray and bake for 20 minutes, turning halfway through. Remove from the oven and reserve.

3 Heat the oil in a large saucepan. Gently cook the onion and garlic for 3–4 minutes.

4 Stir in the ground ginger and cook for 1 minute to release the flavour.

5 Add the chopped carrots, then stir in the stock and the fresh ginger. Simmer gently for 15 minutes.

6 Remove from the heat and allow to cool a little. Blend until smooth, then season to taste with salt and pepper. Stir in the lemon juice. Garnish with the chives and lemon zest and serve immediately.

Nutritional details per 100 g energy 75 kcals/314 kj · protein 3 g · carbohydrate 13 g · fat 2 g · fibre 2 g · sugar 4.3 g · sodium 0.5 g
✓ cows' milk-free   ✓ egg-free   ● gluten-free   ● wheat-free   ✓ nut-free   ✓ vegetarian   ✓ vegan   ✓ seafood-free

Hot Herby Mushrooms

INGREDIENTS

Serves 4

4 thin slices of white bread,
  crusts removed
125 g/4 oz chestnut mushrooms,
  wiped and sliced
125 g/4 oz oyster
  mushrooms, wiped
1 garlic clove, peeled and crushed
1 tsp Dijon mustard
300 ml/½ pint vegetable stock
  salt and freshly ground
  black pepper
1 tbsp freshly chopped parsley
1 tbsp freshly snipped chives,
  plus extra to garnish
mixed salad leaves, to serve

1 Preheat the oven to 180°C/350°F/Gas Mark 4. With a rolling pin, roll each piece of bread out as thinly as possible.

2 Press each piece of bread into a 10 cm/4 inch tartlet tin. Push each piece firmly down, then bake in the preheated oven for 20 minutes.

3 Place the mushrooms in a frying pan with the garlic, mustard and vegetable stock and stir-fry over a moderate heat until the mushrooms are tender and the liquid is reduced by half.

4 Carefully remove the mushrooms from the frying pan with a slotted spoon and transfer to a heat-resistant dish. Cover with tinfoil and place in the bottom of the oven to keep the mushrooms warm.

5 Boil the remaining pan juices until reduced to a thick sauce. Season with salt and pepper.

6 Stir the parsley and the chives into the mushroom mixture.

7 Place one bread tartlet case on each plate and divide the mushroom mixture between them.

8 Spoon over the pan juices, garnish with the chives and serve immediately with mixed salad leaves.

Nutritional details per 100 g · energy 81 kcals/342 kj · protein 4 g · carbohydrate 15 g · fat 1 g · fibre 0.7 g · sugar 1.8 g · sodium 0.5 g

◐ cows' milk-free ✓ egg-free ◐ gluten-free ◐ wheat-free ✓ nut-free ✓ vegetarian ✓ vegan ✓ seafood-free

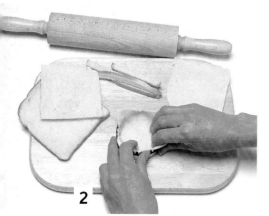
2

3

5

Citrus–grilled Plaice

INGREDIENTS

Serves 4

1 tsp sunflower oil
1 onion, peeled and chopped
1 orange pepper, deseeded
  and chopped
175 g/6 oz long-grain rice
150 ml/¼ pint orange juice
2 tbsp lemon juice
225 ml/8 fl oz vegetable stock
spray of oil
4 x 175 g/6 oz plaice fillets, skinned
1 orange
1 lemon
25 g/1 oz half-fat butter
  or low-fat spread
2 tbsp freshly chopped tarragon
salt and freshly ground
  black pepper
lemon wedges, to garnish

1 Heat the oil in a large frying pan, then sauté the onion, pepper and rice for 2 minutes.

2 Add the orange and lemon juice and bring to the boil. Reduce the heat, add half the stock and simmer for 15–20 minutes, or until the rice is tender, adding the remaining stock as necessary.

3 Preheat the grill. Finely spray the base of the grill pan with oil. Place the plaice fillets in the base and reserve.

4 Finely grate the orange and lemon rind. Squeeze the juice from half of each fruit.

5 Melt the butter or low-fat spread in a small saucepan. Add the grated rind, juice and half of the tarragon and use to baste the plaice fillets.

6 Cook one side only of the fish under the preheated grill at a medium heat for 4–6 minutes, basting continuously.

7 Once the rice is cooked, stir in the remaining tarragon and season to taste with salt and pepper. Garnish the fish with the lemon wedges and serve immediately with the rice.

Nutritional details per 100 g   energy 74 kcals/312 kj · protein 8 g · carbohydrate 8 g · fat 1 g · fibre 0.4 g · sugar 1.4 g · sodium 0.2 g

◑ cows' milk-free   ✓ egg-free   ◑ gluten-free   ◐ wheat-free   ✓ nut-free   ◑ vegetarian   ◐ vegan   ◑ seafood-free

2

4

5

Fusilli Pasta with Spicy Tomato Salsa

INGREDIENTS

Serves 4

6 large ripe tomatoes
2 tbsp lemon juice
2 tbsp lime juice
grated rind of 1 lime
2 shallots, peeled and
  finely chopped
2 garlic cloves, peeled and
  finely chopped
1–2 red chillies
1–2 green chillies
450 g/1 lb fresh fusilli pasta
4 tbsp half-fat crème fraîche
2 tbsp freshly chopped basil
sprig of oregano, to garnish

1 Place the tomatoes in a bowl and cover with boiling water. Allow to stand until the skins start to peel away.

2 Remove the skins from the tomatoes, divide each tomato in four and remove all the seeds. Chop the flesh into small cubes and put in a small pan. Add the lemon and lime juice and the grated lime rind and stir well.

3 Add the chopped shallots and garlic. Remove the seeds carefully from the chillies, chop finely and add to the pan.

4 Bring to the boil and simmer gently for 5–10 minutes until the salsa has thickened slightly.

5 Reserve the salsa to allow the flavours to develop while the pasta is cooking.

6 Bring a large pan of water to the boil and add the pasta. Simmer gently for 3–4 minutes or until the pasta is just tender.

7 Drain the pasta and rinse in boiling water. Top with a large spoonful of salsa and a small spoonful of crème fraîche. Garnish with the chopped basil and oregano and serve immediately.

Nutritional details per 100 g energy 59 kcals/252 kj · protein 3 g · carbohydrate 12 g · fat 0.7 g · fibre 0.6 g · sugar 0.3 g · sodium trace

cows' milk-free · egg-free · gluten-free · wheat-free · ✓ nut-free · ✓ vegetarian · vegan · ✓ seafood-free

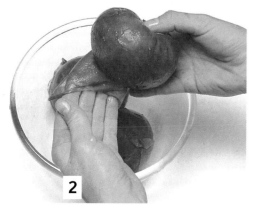

2

3

6

Beef Fajitas with Avocado Sauce

INGREDIENTS

Serves 3–6

2 tbsp sunflower oil

450 g/1 lb beef fillet or rump
  steak, trimmed and cut into
  thin strips

2 garlic cloves, peeled
  and crushed

1 tsp ground cumin

¼ tsp cayenne pepper

1 tbsp paprika

230 g can chopped tomatoes

215 g can red kidney beans, drained

1 tbsp freshly chopped coriander

1 avocado, peeled, pitted
  and chopped

1 shallot, peeled and chopped

1 large tomato, skinned,
  deseeded and chopped

1 red chilli, diced

1 tbsp lemon juice

6 large flour tortilla pancakes

3–4 tbsp soured cream

green salad, to serve

1. Heat the wok, add the oil, then stir-fry the beef for 3–4 minutes. Add the garlic and spices and continue to cook for a further 2 minutes. Stir the tomatoes into the wok, bring to the boil, cover and simmer gently for 5 minutes.

2. Meanwhile, blend the kidney beans in a food processor until slightly broken up, then add to the wok. Continue to cook for a further 5 minutes, adding 2–3 tablespoons of water. The mixture should be thick and fairly dry. Stir in the chopped coriander.

3. Mix the chopped avocado, shallot, tomato, chilli and lemon juice together. Spoon into a serving dish and reserve.

4. When ready to serve, warm the tortillas and spread with a little soured cream. Place a spoonful of the beef mixture on top, followed by a spoonful of the avocado sauce, then roll up. Repeat until all the mixture is used up. Serve immediately with a green salad.

Nutritional details per 100 g energy 177 kcals/740 kj · protein 11 g · carbohydrate 16 g · fat 8 g · fibre 1.2 g · sugar 1.4 g · sodium 0.2 g

◐ cows' milk-free   ✓ egg-free   ◐ gluten-free   ◐ wheat-free   ✓ nut-free   ◐ vegetarian   ◐ vegan   ✓ seafood-free

Lamb Meatballs with Savoy Cabbage

INGREDIENTS

Serves 4

450 g/1 lb fresh lamb mince
1 tbsp freshly chopped parsley
1 tbsp freshly grated root ginger
1 tbsp light soy sauce
1 medium egg yolk
4 tbsp dark soy sauce
2 tbsp dry sherry
1 tbsp cornflour
3 tbsp vegetable oil
2 garlic cloves, peeled and chopped
1 bunch spring onions, trimmed
  and shredded
½ Savoy cabbage, trimmed
  and shredded
½ head Chinese leaves, trimmed
  and shredded
freshly chopped red chilli,
  to garnish

1 Place the lamb mince in a large bowl with the parsley, ginger, light soy sauce and egg yolk and mix together. Divide the mixture into walnut-sized pieces and, using your hands, roll into balls. Place on a baking sheet, cover with clingfilm and chill in the refrigerator for at least 30 minutes.

2 Meanwhile, blend together the dark soy sauce, sherry and cornflour with 2 tablespoons of water in a small bowl until smooth. Reserve.

3 Heat a wok, add the oil and when hot, add the meatballs and cook for 5–8 minutes, or until browned all over, turning occasionally. Using a slotted spoon, transfer the meatballs to a large plate and keep warm.

4 Add the garlic, spring onions, Savoy cabbage and the Chinese leaves to the wok and stir-fry for 3 minutes. Pour over the reserved soy sauce mixture, bring to the boil, then simmer for 30 seconds or until thickened. Return the meatballs to the wok and mix in. Garnish with chopped red chilli and serve immediately.

Nutritional details per 100 g energy 105 kcals/437 kj · protein 8 g · carbohydrate 5 g · fat 6 g · fibre trace · sugar 0.4 g · sodium 0.3 g

✓ cows' milk-free ◖ egg-free ◖ gluten-free ◖ wheat-free ✓ nut-free ◖ vegetarian ◖ vegan ✓ seafood-free

1

3

4

Pasta Shells with Broccoli & Capers

INGREDIENTS

Serves 4

400 g/14 oz conchiglie (shells)

450 g/1 lb broccoli florets, cut into
   small pieces

5 tbsp olive oil

1 large onion, peeled and
   finely chopped

4 tbsp capers in brine, rinsed
   and drained

½ tsp dried chilli flakes (optional)

75 g/3 oz freshly grated
   Parmesan cheese, plus
   extra to serve

25 g/1 oz pecorino cheese, grated

salt and freshly ground black pepper

2 tbsp freshly chopped flat-leaf
   parsley, to garnish

1 Bring a large pan of lightly salted water to a rolling boil. Add the pasta shells, return to the boil and cook for 2 minutes. Add the broccoli to the pan. Return to the boil and continue cooking for 8–10 minutes, or until the conchiglie is 'al dente'.

2 Meanwhile, heat the olive oil in a large frying pan, add the onion and cook for 5 minutes, or until softened, stirring frequently. Stir in the capers and chilli flakes, if using, and cook for a further 2 minutes.

3 Drain the pasta and broccoli and add to the frying pan. Toss the ingredients to mix thoroughly. Sprinkle over the cheeses, then stir until the cheeses have just melted. Season to taste with salt and pepper, then tip into a warmed serving dish. Garnish with chopped parsley and serve immediately with extra Parmesan cheese.

Nutritional details per 100 g energy 136 kcals/569 kj · protein 6 g · carbohydrate 12 g · fat 7 g · fibre 1.7 g · sugar 1.6 g · sodium 0.2 g

  cows' milk-free   egg-free   gluten-free   wheat-free   ✓ nut-free   ✓ vegetarian   vegan   ✓ seafood-free

Stir–fried Greens

INGREDIENTS

Serves 4

450 g/1 lb Chinese leaves
225 g/8 oz pak choi
225 g/8 oz broccoli florets
1 tbsp sesame seeds
1 tbsp groundnut oil
1 tbsp fresh root ginger, peeled
  and finely chopped
3 garlic cloves, peeled and
  finely chopped
2 red chillies, deseeded and
  split in half
50 ml/2 fl oz vegetable stock
2 tbsp Chinese rice wine
1 tbsp dark soy sauce
1 tsp light soy sauce
2 tsp black bean sauce
freshly ground black pepper
2 tsp sugar
1 tsp sesame oil

1 Separate the Chinese leaves and pak choi and wash well. Cut into 2.5 cm/1 inch strips. Separate the broccoli into small florets. Heat a wok or large frying pan, add the sesame seeds and stir-fry for 30 seconds or until browned.

2 Add the oil to the wok and when hot, add the ginger, garlic and chillies and stir-fry for 30 seconds. Add the broccoli and stir-fry for 1 minute. Add the Chinese leaves and pak choi and stir-fry for a further 1 minute.

3 Pour the vegetable stock and Chinese rice wine into the wok with the soy and black bean sauces. Season to taste with pepper and add the sugar. Reduce the heat and simmer for 6–8 minutes, or until the vegetables are tender but still firm to the bite. Tip into a warmed serving dish, removing the chillies if preferred. Drizzle with the sesame oil and serve immediately.

Nutritional details per 100 g energy 38 kcals/158 kj · protein 2 g · carbohydrate 5 g · fat 2 g · fibre trace g · sugar 1 g · sodium 0.2 g

✓ cows' milk-free   ✓ egg-free   ◐ gluten-free   ◐ wheat-free   ◐ nut-free   ✓ vegetarian   ✓ vegan   ✓ seafood-free

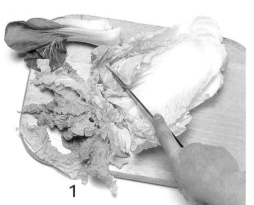

1

2

3

Rice & Papaya Salad

INGREDIENTS

Serves 4

175 g/6 oz easy-cook basmati rice

1 cinnamon stick, bruised

1 bird's-eye chilli, deseeded
  and finely chopped

rind and juice of 2 limes

rind and juice of 2 lemons

2 tbsp Thai fish sauce

1 tbsp soft light brown sugar

1 papaya, peeled and seeds removed

1 mango, peeled and stone removed

1 green chilli, deseeded and
  finely chopped

2 tbsp freshly chopped coriander

1 tbsp freshly chopped mint

250 g/9 oz cooked chicken

50 g/2 oz roasted peanuts, chopped

strips of pitta bread, to serve

1. Rinse and drain the rice and pour into a saucepan. Add 450 ml/ ¾ pint of boiling salted water and the cinnamon stick. Bring to the boil, reduce to a very low heat, then cover and cook without stirring for 15–18 minutes, or until all the liquid is absorbed. The rice should be light and fluffy and have steam holes on the surface. Remove the cinnamon stick and stir in the rind from 1 lime.

2. To make the dressing, place the bird's-eye chilli, remaining rind and lime and lemon juice, fish sauce and sugar in a food processor and mix until blended. Alternatively, place all the ingredients in a screw-top jar and shake until mixed. Pour half the dressing over the hot rice and toss until the rice glistens.

3. Slice the papaya and mango into thin slices, then place in a bowl. Add the chopped green chilli, coriander and mint. Place the chicken onto a chopping board, then remove and discard any skin or sinews. Cut into fine shreds and add to the bowl with the chopped peanuts.

4. Add the remaining dressing to the chicken mixture and stir until all the ingredients are lightly coated. Spoon the rice onto a platter, pile the chicken mixture on top and serve with warm strips of pitta bread.

Nutritional details per 100 g   energy 108 kcals/455 kj · protein 8 g · carbohydrate 17 g · fat 2 g · fibre 0.4 g · sugar 1.7 g · sodium trace

✓ cows' milk-free   ✓ egg-free   ◖ gluten-free   ◖ wheat-free   ◖ nut-free   ◖ vegetarian   ◖ vegan   ◖ seafood-free

1

3

3

Vegetables Braised in Olive Oil & Lemon

INGREDIENTS

Serves 4

small strip of pared rind
    and juice of ½ lemon
4 tbsp olive oil
1 bay leaf
large sprig of thyme
150 ml/¼ pint water
4 spring onions, trimmed and
    finely chopped
175 g/6 oz baby button mushrooms
175 g/6 oz broccoli, cut into
    small florets
175 g/6 oz cauliflower, cut into
    small florets
1 medium courgette, sliced on
    the diagonal
2 tbsp freshly snipped chives
salt and freshly ground
    black pepper
lemon zest, to garnish

1 Put the pared lemon rind and juice into a large saucepan. Add the olive oil, bay leaf, thyme and the water. Bring to the boil. Add the spring onions and mushrooms. Top with the broccoli and cauliflower, trying to add them so that the stalks are submerged in the water and the tops are just above it. Cover and simmer for 3 minutes.

2 Scatter the courgettes on top, so that they are steamed rather than boiled. Cook, covered, for a further 3–4 minutes, until all the vegetables are tender. Using a slotted spoon, transfer the vegetables from the liquid into a warmed serving dish. Increase the heat and boil rapidly for 3–4 minutes, or until the liquid is reduced to about 8 tablespoons. Remove the lemon rind, bay leaf and thyme sprig and discard.

3 Stir the chives into the reduced liquid, season to taste with salt and pepper and pour over the vegetables. Sprinkle with lemon zest and serve immediately.

Nutritional details per 100 g   energy 72 kcals/297 kj · protein 2 g · carbohydrate 2 g · fat 6 g · fibre 1.4 g · sugar 1.1 g · sodium trace

✓ cows' milk-free   ✓ egg-free   ✓ gluten-free   ✓ wheat-free   ✓ nut-free   ✓ vegetarian   ✓ vegan   ✓ seafood-free

Wild Garlic Mushrooms with Pizza Breadsticks

INGREDIENTS

Serves 6

For the breadsticks:

7 g/¼ oz dried yeast
250 ml/8 fl oz warm water
400 g/14 oz strong, plain flour
2 tbsp olive oil
1 tsp salt

For the mushrooms:

9 tbsp olive oil
4 garlic cloves, peeled
  and crushed
450 g/1 lb mixed wild mushrooms,
  wiped and dried
salt and freshly ground
  black pepper
1 tbsp freshly chopped parsley
1 tbsp freshly chopped basil
1 tsp fresh oregano leaves
juice of 1 lemon

1 Preheat the oven to 240°C/475°F/Gas Mark 9, 15 minutes before baking. Place the dried yeast in the warm water for 10 minutes. Place the flour in a large bowl and gradually blend in the olive oil, salt and the dissolved yeast.

2 Knead on a lightly floured surface to form a smooth and pliable dough. Cover with clingfilm and leave in a warm place for 15 minutes to allow the dough to rise, then roll out again and cut into sticks of equal length. Cover and leave to rise again for 10 minutes. Brush with the olive oil, sprinkle with salt and bake in the preheated oven for 10 minutes.

3 Pour 3 tablespoons of the oil into a frying pan and add the crushed garlic. Cook over a very low heat, stirring well for 3–4 minutes to flavour the oil.

4 Cut the wild mushrooms into bite-sized slices if very large, then add to the pan. Season well with salt and pepper and cook very gently for 6–8 minutes, or until tender.

5 Whisk the fresh herbs, the remaining olive oil and lemon juice together. Pour over the mushrooms and heat through. Season to taste and place on individual serving dishes. Serve with the pizza breadsticks.

Nutritional details per 100 g   energy 249 kcals/1045 kj · protein 6 g · carbohydrate 32 g · fat 12 g · fibre 1.3 g · sugar 0.6 g · sodium 0.2 g

✓ cows' milk-free   ✓ egg-free   ◐ gluten-free   ◐ wheat-free   ✓ nut-free   ✓ vegetarian   ✓ vegan   ✓ seafood-free

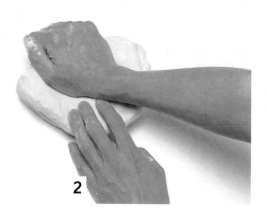

2

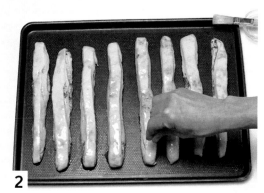

2

= 4

Autumn Fruit Layer

INGREDIENTS

Serves 4

450 g/1 lb Bramley
   cooking apples
225 g/8 oz blackberries
50 g/2 oz soft brown sugar
juice of 1 lemon
50 g/2 oz low-fat spread
200 g/7 oz breadcrumbs
225 g/8 oz honey-coated nut
   mix, chopped
redcurrants and mint leaves,
   to decorate
half-fat whipped cream or
   reduced-fat ice cream,
   to serve

1 Peel, core and slice the cooking apples and place in a saucepan with the blackberries, sugar and lemon juice.

2 Cover the fruit mixture and simmer, stirring occasionally for about 15 minutes or until the apples and blackberries have formed a thick purée.

3 Remove the pan from the heat and allow to cool.

4 Melt the low-fat spread in a frying pan and cook the breadcrumbs for 5–10 minutes, stirring occasionally until golden and crisp.

5 Remove the pan from the heat and stir in the nuts. Allow to cool.

6 Alternately layer the fruit purée and breadcrumbs into four tall glasses.

7 Store the desserts in the refrigerator to chill and remove when ready to serve.

8 Decorate with redcurrants and mint leaves and serve with half-fat whipped cream or a reduced-fat vanilla or raspberry ice cream.

Nutritional details per 100 g   energy 198 kcals/828 kj · protein 4 g · carbohydrate 27 g · fat 9 g · fibre 1.8 g · sugar 15.6 g · sodium 0.2 g

◗ cows' milk-free   ◗ egg-free   ◗ gluten-free   ◗ wheat-free   ◗ nut-free   ✓ vegetarian   ◗ vegan   ✓ seafood-free

Summer Fruit Semifreddo

INGREDIENTS

Serves 6–8

225 g/8 oz raspberries
125 g/4 oz blueberries
125 g/4 oz redcurrants
50 g/2 oz icing sugar
juice of 1 lemon
1 vanilla pod, split
50 g/2 oz sugar
4 large eggs, separated
600 ml/1 pint double cream
pinch of salt
fresh redcurrants, to decorate

1   Wash and hull or remove stalks from the fruits, as necessary, then put them into a food processor or blender with the icing sugar and lemon juice. Blend to a purée, pour into a jug and chill in the refrigerator, until needed.

2   Remove the seeds from the vanilla pod by opening the pod and scraping with the back of a knife. Add the seeds to the sugar and whisk with the egg yolks until pale and thick.

3   In another bowl, whip the cream until soft peaks form. Do not overwhip. In a third bowl, whip the egg whites with the salt until stiff peaks form.

4   Using a large metal spoon – to avoid knocking any air from the mixture – fold together the fruit purée, egg yolk mixture, the cream and egg whites. Transfer the mixture to a round, shallow, lidded freezer box and put into the freezer until almost frozen. If the mixture freezes solid, thaw in the refrigerator until semi-frozen. Turn out the semi-frozen mixture, cut into wedges and serve decorated with a few fresh redcurrants. If the mixture thaws completely, eat immediately and do not refreeze.

Nutritional details per 100 g   energy 309 kcals/1277 kj · protein 3 g · carbohydrate 9 g · fat 29 g · fibre 0.6 g · sugar 5 g · sodium trace

◖ cows' milk-free   ◖ egg-free   ✓ gluten-free   ✓ wheat-free   ✓ nut-free   ✓ vegetarian   ◖ vegan   ✓ seafood-free

1

2

4

High Blood Pressure

High Blood Pressure has been linked to life endangering health problems such as strokes, heart attacks and blood clots. This section provides recipes that are low in salt and fat (which can increase the chance of high blood pressure) and high in fibre and essential oils (which can help to prevent it). These healthier meals still retain their taste and are easy to prepare.

Citrus Monkfish Kebabs

INGREDIENTS

Serves 4

For the marinade:

1 tbsp sunflower oil
finely grated rind and juice
    of 1 lime
1 tbsp lemon juice
1 sprig of freshly
    chopped rosemary
1 tbsp wholegrain mustard
1 garlic clove, peeled
    and crushed
freshly ground black pepper

For the kebabs:

450 g/1 lb monkfish tail
8 raw tiger prawns
1 small green courgette, trimmed
    and sliced
4 tbsp of half-fat
    crème fraîche

1 Preheat the grill and line the grill rack with tinfoil. Mix all the marinade ingredients together in a small bowl and reserve.

2 Using a sharp knife, cut down both sides of the monkfish tail. Remove the bone and discard. Cut away and discard any skin, then cut the monkfish into bite-sized cubes.

3 Peel the prawns, leaving the tails intact and remove the thin black vein that runs down the back of each prawn. Place the fish and prawns in a shallow dish.

4 Pour the marinade over the fish and prawns. Cover lightly and leave to marinate in the refrigerator for 30 minutes. Spoon the marinade over the fish and prawns occasionally during this time. Soak the skewers in cold water for 30 minutes, then drain.

5 Thread the cubes of fish, prawns and courgettes onto the drained skewers.

6 Arrange on the grill rack then place under the preheated grill and cook for 5–7 minutes, or until cooked thoroughly and the prawns have turned pink. Occasionally brush with the remaining marinade and turn the kebabs during cooking.

7 Mix 2 tablespoons of marinade with the crème fraîche and serve as a dip with the kebabs.

Nutritional details per 100 g   energy 95 kcals/396 kj · protein 15 g · carbohydrate 2 g · fat 3 g · fibre 0.2 g · sugar 0.3 g · sodium 0.2 g

◖ cows' milk-free   ✓ egg-free   ◖ gluten-free   ◖ wheat-free   ✓ nut-free   ◖ vegetarian   ◖ vegan   ◖ seafood-free

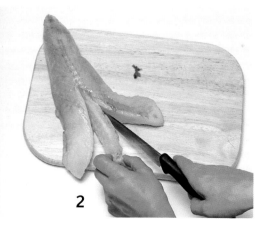

2

4

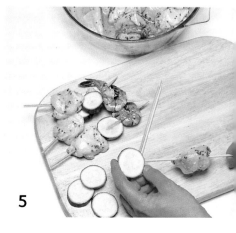

5

Bulghur Wheat Salad with Minty Lemon Dressing

INGREDIENTS

Serves 4

125 g/4 oz bulghur wheat
10 cm /4 inch piece cucumber
2 shallots, peeled
125 g/4 oz baby sweetcorn
3 ripe but firm tomatoes

For the dressing:

grated rind of 1 lemon
3 tbsp lemon juice
3 tbsp freshly chopped mint
2 tbsp freshly chopped parsley
1–2 tsp clear honey
2 tbsp sunflower oil
freshly ground black pepper

1 Place the bulghur wheat in a saucepan and cover with boiling water.

2 Simmer for about 10 minutes, then drain thoroughly and turn into a serving bowl.

3 Cut the cucumber into small cubes, chop the shallots finely and reserve. Steam the sweetcorn over a pan of boiling water for 10 minutes or until tender. Drain and slice into thick chunks.

4 Cut a cross on the top of each tomato and place in boiling water until their skins start to peel away.

5 Remove the skins and the seeds and cut the tomatoes into small cubes.

6 Make the dressing by briskly whisking all the ingredients in a small bowl until mixed well.

7 When the bulghur wheat has cooled a little, add all the prepared vegetables and stir in the dressing. Season to taste with pepper and serve.

Nutritional details per 100 g · energy 65 kcals/270 kj · protein 2 g · carbohydrate 8 g · fat 3 g · fibre 0.8 g · sugar 3.4 g · sodium 0.3 g

✓ cows' milk-free   ✓ egg-free   ✓ gluten-free   ✓ wheat-free   ✓ nut-free   ✓ vegetarian   ✓ vegan   ✓ seafood-free

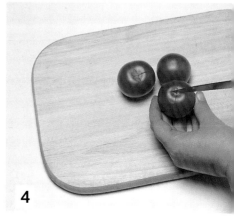

Chicken Noodle Soup

INGREDIENTS

Serves 4

carcass of a medium-sized
  cooked chicken
1 large carrot, peeled and
  roughly chopped
1 medium onion, peeled
  and quartered
1 leek, trimmed and roughly chopped
2–3 bay leaves
a few black peppercorns
2 litres/3½ pints water
225 g/8 oz Chinese cabbage, trimmed
50 g/2 oz chestnut mushrooms,
  wiped and sliced
125 g/4 oz cooked chicken,
  sliced or chopped
50 g/2 oz medium or fine egg
  thread noodles

1 Break the chicken carcass into smaller pieces and place in a wok with the carrot, onion, leek, bay leaves, peppercorns and water. Bring slowly to the boil. Skim away any fat or scum that rises for the first 15 minutes. Simmer very gently for 1–1½ hours. If the liquid reduces by more than one third, add a little more water.

2 Remove from the heat and leave until cold. Strain into a large bowl and chill in the refrigerator until any fat in the stock rises and sets on the surface. Remove the fat and discard. Draw a sheet of absorbent kitchen paper across the surface of the stock to absorb any remaining fat.

3 Return the stock to the wok and bring to a simmer. Add the Chinese cabbage, mushrooms and chicken and simmer gently for 7–8 minutes until the vegetables are tender.

4 Meanwhile, cook the noodles according to the packet directions until tender. Drain well. Transfer a portion of noodles to each serving bowl before pouring in some soup and vegetables. Serve immediately.

Nutritional details per 100 g energy 43 kcals/182 kj · protein 5 g · carbohydrate 4 g · fat 0.8 g · fibre 0.9 g · sugar 2.1 g · sodium trace

✓ cows' milk-free   ◖ egg-free   ◖ gluten-free   ◖ wheat-free   ✓ nut-free   ◖ vegetarian   ◖ vegan   ✓ seafood-free

Chinese Salad with Soy & Ginger Dressing

INGREDIENTS

Serves 4

1 head of Chinese cabbage
200 g can water chestnuts, drained
6 spring onions, trimmed
4 ripe but firm cherry tomatoes
125 g/4 oz mangetout
125 g/4 oz beansprouts
2 tbsp freshly chopped coriander

For the soy and ginger dressing:

2 tbsp sunflower oil
2 tbsp light soy sauce
2.5 cm/1 inch piece root ginger,
   peeled and finely grated
zest and juice of 1 lemon
freshly ground black pepper
crusty white bread,
   to serve

1. Rinse and finely shred the Chinese cabbage and place in a serving dish.

2. Slice the water chestnuts into small slivers and cut the spring onions diagonally into 2.5 cm/1 inch lengths, then split lengthways into thin strips.

3. Cut the tomatoes in half and then slice each half into three wedges and reserve.

4. Simmer the mangetout in boiling water for 2 minutes until beginning to soften, drain and cut in half diagonally.

5. Arrange the water chestnuts, spring onions, mangetout, tomatoes and beansprouts on top of the shredded Chinese cabbage. Garnish with the freshly chopped coriander.

6. Make the dressing by whisking all the ingredients together in a small bowl until mixed thoroughly. Serve with the bread and the salad.

Nutritional details per 100 g   energy 73 kcals/306 kj · protein 2 g · carbohydrate 12 g · fat 2 g · fibre 0.6 g · sugar 1.2 g · sodium 0.5 g

✓ cows' milk-free   ✓ egg-free   ◐ gluten-free   ◐ wheat-free   ✓ nut-free   ✓ vegetarian   ✓ vegan   ◐ seafood-free

2

3

5

Chunky Halibut Casserole

INGREDIENTS

Serves 6

1 tbsp olive oil

2 large onions, peeled and
sliced into rings

1 red pepper, deseeded and
roughly chopped

450 g/1 lb potatoes, peeled

450 g/1 lb courgettes, trimmed
and thickly sliced

2 tbsp plain flour

1 tbsp paprika

2 tsp vegetable oil

150 ml/¼ pint fish stock

400 g can chopped tomatoes

2 tbsp freshly chopped basil

freshly ground black pepper

450 g/1 lb halibut fillet,
skinned and cut into
2.5 cm/1 inch cubes

sprigs of fresh basil,
to garnish

freshly cooked rice,
to serve

1 Heat the oil in a large saucepan, add the onions and pepper and cook for 5 minutes, or until softened.

2 Cut the peeled potatoes into 2.5 cm/1 inch cubes, rinse lightly and shake dry, then add them to the onions and pepper in the saucepan. Add the courgettes and cook, stirring frequently, for a further 2–3 minutes.

3 Sprinkle the flour, paprika and vegetable oil into the saucepan and cook, stirring continuously, for 1 minute. Pour in the stock and the chopped tomatoes, and bring to the boil.

4 Add the basil to the casserole, season to taste with pepper and cover. Simmer for 15 minutes, then add the halibut and simmer very gently for a further 5–7 minutes, or until the fish and vegetables are just tender.

5 Garnish with basil sprigs and serve immediately with freshly cooked rice.

Nutritional details per 100 g energy 72 kcals/307 kj · protein 6 g · carbohydrate 11 g · fat 1 g · fibre 0.9 g · sugar 2.1 g · sodium trace

✓ cows' milk-free   ✓ egg-free   ◐ gluten-free   ◐ wheat-free   ✓ nut-free   ◐ vegetarian   ◐ vegan   ◐ seafood-free

Pad Thai

INGREDIENTS

Serves 4

225 g/8 oz flat rice noodles

2 tbsp vegetable oil

225 g/8 oz boneless chicken breast,
   skinned and thinly sliced

4 shallots, peeled and thinly sliced

2 garlic cloves, peeled and
   finely chopped

4 spring onions, trimmed
   and diagonally cut into
   5 cm/2 inch pieces

350 g/12 oz fresh white crab meat
   or tiny prawns

75 g/3 oz fresh bean sprouts,
   rinsed and drained

2 tbsp preserved or fresh radish

2–3 tbsp roasted peanuts,
   chopped (optional)

For the sauce:

2 tbsp Thai fish sauce (nam pla)

2–3 tbsp rice vinegar or cider vinegar

1 tbsp chilli bean or oyster sauce

1 tbsp toasted sesame oil

1 tbsp light brown sugar

1 red chilli, deseeded and thinly sliced

1 To make the sauce, whisk all the sauce ingredients in a bowl and reserve. Put the rice noodles in a large bowl and pour over enough hot water to cover. Leave to stand for about 15 minutes until softened. Drain and rinse, then drain again.

2 Heat the oil in a wok over a high heat until hot, but not smoking. Add the chicken strips and stir-fry constantly until they begin to colour. Using a slotted spoon, transfer to a plate. Reduce the heat to medium-high.

3 Add the shallots, garlic and spring onions and stir-fry for 1 minute. Stir in the rice noodles, then the reserved sauce and mix well.

4 Add the reserved chicken strips with the crab meat or prawns, bean sprouts and radish and stir well. Cook for about 5 minutes, stirring frequently, until heated through. If the noodles begin to stick, add a little water.

5 Turn into a large, shallow serving dish and sprinkle with the chopped peanuts, if using. Serve immediately.

Nutritional details per 100 g   energy 129 kcals/540 kj · protein 13 g · carbohydrate 8 g · fat 5 g · fibre 0.5 g · sugar 2.3 g · sodium 0.6 g

✓ cows' milk-free   ✓ egg-free   ◖ gluten-free   ◖ wheat-free   ◖ nut-free   ◖ vegetarian   ◖ vegan   ◖ seafood-free

1

2

3

Rice with Squash & Sage

INGREDIENTS

Serves 4–6

450 g/1 lb butternut squash
2 tbsp olive oil
1 small onion, peeled and
  finely chopped
3 garlic cloves, peeled and crushed
2 tbsp freshly chopped sage
1 litre/1 ³/₄ pints vegetable stock
450 g/1 lb Arborio rice
50 g/2 oz pine nuts, toasted
freshly snipped chives,
  to garnish
freshly ground black pepper

1 Peel the squash, cut in half lengthways and remove the seeds and stringy flesh. Cut remaining flesh into small cubes and reserve.

2 Heat the wok, add the oil and heat until bubbling, then add the onion, garlic and sage and stir-fry for 1 minute.

3 Add the squash to the wok and stir-fry for a further 10–12 minutes, or until the squash is tender. Remove from the heat.

4 Meanwhile, bring the vegetable stock to the boil and add the rice. Cook for 8–10 minutes, or until the rice is just tender but still quite wet.

5 Add the cooked rice to the squash mixture. Stir in the pine nuts and season to taste with pepper. Garnish with snipped chives and serve immediately.

Nutritional details per 100 g energy 107 kcals/446 kj · protein 2 g · carbohydrate 14 g · fat 5 g · fibre 0.2 g · sugar 0.6 g · sodium 0.3 g
✓ cows' milk-free   ✓ egg-free   ◖ gluten-free   ◖ wheat-free   ◖ nut-free   ✓ vegetarian   ✓ vegan   ✓ seafood-free

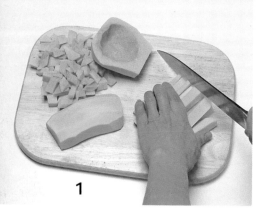

1

2

5

Salmon Noisettes with Fruity Sauce

INGREDIENTS

Serves 4

4 x 125 g/4 oz salmon steaks
grated rind and juice of
  2 lemons
grated rind and juice of
  1 lime
3 tbsp olive oil
1 tbsp clear honey
1 tbsp wholegrain mustard
freshly ground black pepper
1 tbsp sunflower oil
125 g/4 oz mixed salad
  leaves, washed
1 bunch watercress, washed and
  thick stalks removed
250 g/9 oz baby plum
  tomatoes, halved

1　Using a sharp knife, cut the bone away from each salmon steak to create two salmon fillets. Repeat with the remaining salmon steaks. Shape the salmon fillets into noisettes and secure with fine string.

2　Mix together the citrus rinds and juices, olive oil, honey, wholegrain mustard and pepper in a shallow dish. Add the salmon fillets and turn to coat. Cover and leave to marinate in the refrigerator for 4 hours, turning them occasionally in the marinade.

3　Heat the wok then add the sunflower oil and heat until hot. Lift out the salmon noisettes, reserving the marinade. Add the salmon to the wok and cook for 6–10 minutes, turning once during cooking, until the fish is cooked through and just flaking. Pour the marinade into the wok and heat through gently.

4　Mix together the salad leaves, watercress and tomatoes and arrange on serving plates. Top with the salmon noisettes and drizzle over any remaining warm marinade. Serve immediately.

Nutritional details per 100 g energy 129 kcals/537 kj · protein 10 g · carbohydrate 5 g · fat 9 g · fibre 0.3 g · sugar 2 g · sodium trace

✓ cows' milk-free ✓ egg-free ◖ gluten-free ◖ wheat-free ✓ nut-free ◖ vegetarian ◖ vegan ◖ seafood-free

1

2

3

Salmon with Herbed Potatoes

INGREDIENTS

Serves 4

450 g/1 lb baby new potatoes

freshly ground black pepper

4 salmon steaks, each weighing
  about 175 g/6 oz

1 carrot, peeled and cut into
  fine strips

175 g/6 oz asparagus
  spears, trimmed

175 g/6 oz sugar snap
  peas, trimmed

finely grated rind and juice
  of 1 lemon

1 tbsp olive oil

4 large sprigs of fresh parsley

1. Preheat the oven to 190°C/375°F/Gas Mark 5, about 10 minutes before required. Parboil the potatoes in lightly salted boiling water for 5–8 minutes until they are barely tender. Drain and reserve.

2. Cut out four pieces of baking parchment paper, measuring 20.5 cm/8 inches square, and place on the work surface. Arrange the parboiled potatoes on top. Wipe the salmon steaks and place on top of the potatoes.

3. Place the carrot strips in a bowl with the asparagus spears, sugar snaps and grated lemon rind and juice. Season to taste with salt and pepper. Toss lightly together.

4. Divide the vegetables evenly between the salmon parcels. Drizzle the top of each parcel with olive oil and add a sprig of parsley.

5. To wrap a parcel, lift up two opposite sides of the paper and fold the edges together. Twist the paper at the other two ends to seal the parcel well. Repeat with the remaining parcels.

6. Place the parcels on a baking tray and bake in the preheated oven for 15 minutes. Place an unopened parcel on each plate and open just before eating.

Nutritional details per 100 g   energy 111 kcals/464 kj · protein 10 g · carbohydrate 6 g · fat 6 g · fibre 1.1 g · sugar 0.9 g · sodium trace

✓ cows' milk-free   ✓ egg-free   ✓ gluten-free   ✓ wheat-free   ✓ nut-free   ✓ vegetarian   vegan   seafood-free

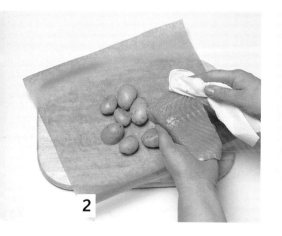

2

3

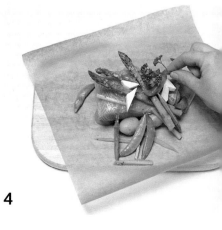

4

Spicy Cucumber Stir Fry

INGREDIENTS

Serves 4

25 g/1 oz black soya
  beans, soaked in cold
  water, overnight
1½ cucumbers
1 tbsp vegetable oil
½ tsp mild chilli powder
4 garlic cloves, peeled
  and crushed
5 tbsp vegetable stock
1 tsp sesame oil
1 tbsp freshly chopped
  parsley, to garnish

1 Rinse the soaked beans thoroughly, then drain. Place in a saucepan, cover with cold water and bring to the boil, skimming off any scum that rises to the surface. Boil for 10 minutes, then reduce the heat and simmer for 1–1½ hours. Drain and reserve.

2 Peel the cucumbers, slice lengthways and remove the seeds. Cut into 2.5 cm/1 inch slices.

3 Heat a wok or large frying pan, add the oil and when hot, add the chilli powder, garlic and black beans and stir-fry for 30 seconds.

4 Add the cucumber and stir-fry for 20 seconds.

5 Pour the stock into the wok and cook for 3–4 minutes, or until the cucumber is very tender. The liquid will have evaporated at this stage.

6 Remove from the heat and stir in the sesame oil. Turn into a warmed serving dish, garnish with chopped parsley and serve immediately.

Nutritional details per 100 g energy 61 kcals/251 kj · protein 2 g · carbohydrate 3 g · fat 5 g · fibre 0.6 g · sugar 0.2 g · sodium 0.2 g

✓ cows' milk-free   ✓ egg-free   ◖ gluten-free   ◖ wheat-free   ✓ nut-free   ◖ vegetarian   ✓ vegan   ◖ seafood-free

1

2

3

Stir–fried Chicken with Spinach, Tomatoes & Pine Nuts

INGREDIENTS

Serves 4

50 g/2 oz pine nuts

2 tbsp sunflower oil

1 red onion, peeled and
  finely chopped

450 g/1 lb skinless, boneless
  chicken breast fillets,
  cut into strips

450 g/1 lb cherry
  tomatoes, halved

225 g/8 oz baby
  spinach, washed

freshly ground black pepper

¼ tsp freshly grated nutmeg

2 tbsp balsamic vinegar

50 g/2 oz raisins

freshly cooked ribbon noodles,
  to serve

1 Heat the wok and add the pine nuts. Dry-fry for about 2 minutes, shaking often to ensure that they toast but do not burn. Remove and reserve. Wipe any dust from the wok.

2 Heat the wok again, add the oil and when hot, add the red onion and stir-fry for 2 minutes. Add the chicken and stir-fry for 2–3 minutes, or until golden brown. Reduce the heat, toss in the cherry tomatoes and stir-fry gently until the tomatoes start to disintegrate.

3 Add the baby spinach and stir-fry for 2–3 minutes, or until they start to wilt. Season to taste with pepper, then sprinkle in the grated nutmeg and drizzle in the balsamic vinegar. Finally, stir in the raisins and reserved toasted pine nuts. Serve immediately on a bed of ribbon noodles.

Nutritional details per 100 g   energy 120 kcals/503 kj · protein 10 g · carbohydrate 9 g · fat 5 g · fibre 1.2 g · sugar 3.7 g · sodium trace

✓ cows' milk-free   ✓ egg-free   ◖ gluten-free   ◖ wheat-free   ◖ nut-free   ◖ vegetarian   ◖ vegan   ✓ seafood-free

Sardines with Redcurrants

INGREDIENTS

Serves 4

2 tbsp redcurrant jelly
finely grated rind of 1 lime
2 tbsp medium dry sherry
450 g/1 lb fresh sardines,
  cleaned and heads removed
freshly ground black pepper
lime wedges, to garnish

To serve:
fresh redcurrants
fresh green salad

1 Preheat the grill and line the grill rack with tinfoil 2–3 minutes before cooking.

2 Warm the redcurrant jelly in a bowl standing over a pan of gently simmering water and stir until smooth. Add the lime rind and sherry to the bowl and stir well until blended.

3 Lightly rinse the sardines and pat dry with absorbent kitchen paper.

4 Place on a chopping board and with a sharp knife make several diagonal cuts across the flesh of each fish. Season the sardines inside the cavities with pepper.

5 Gently brush the warm marinade over the skin and inside the cavities of the sardines.

6 Place on the grill rack and cook under the preheated grill for 8–10 minutes, or until the fish are cooked.

7 Carefully turn the sardines over at least once during grilling. Baste occasionally with the remaining redcurrant and lime marinade. Garnish with the redcurrants and serve immediately with the salad and lime wedges.

Nutritional details per 100 g energy 137 kcals/573 kj · protein 13 g · carbohydrate 7 g · fat 7 g · fibre 0.2 g · sugar 5 g · sodium 0.1 g

✓ cows' milk-free   ✓ egg-free   ✓ gluten-free   ✓ wheat-free   ✓ nut-free   vegetarian   vegan   seafood-free

1

4

5

Turkey & Tomato Tagine

INGREDIENTS

Serves 4

For the meatballs:
450 g/1 lb fresh turkey mince
1 small onion, peeled and very
 finely chopped
1 garlic clove, peeled and crushed
1 tbsp freshly chopped coriander
1 tsp ground cumin
1 tbsp olive oil
freshly ground black pepper

For the sauce:
1 onion, peeled and finely chopped
1 garlic clove, peeled and crushed
150 ml/¹/₄ pint turkey stock
400 g can chopped tomatoes
¹/₂ tsp ground cumin
¹/₂ tsp ground cinnamon
pinch of cayenne pepper
freshly chopped parsley
freshly chopped herbs, to garnish
freshly cooked couscous or rice,
 to serve

1 Preheat the oven to 190°C/375°F/Gas Mark 5. Put all the ingredients for the meatballs in a bowl, except the oil and mix well. Season to taste with salt and pepper. Shape into 20 balls, about the size of walnuts.

2 Put on a tray, cover lightly and chill in the refrigerator while making the sauce.

3 Put the onion and garlic in a pan with 125 ml/4 fl oz of the stock. Cook over a low heat until all the stock has evaporated. Continue cooking for 1 minute, or until the onions begin to colour.

4 Add the remaining stock to the pan with the tomatoes, cumin, cinnamon and cayenne pepper. Simmer for 10 minutes, until slightly thickened and reduced. Stir in the parsley and season to taste.

5 Heat the oil in a large, non-stick frying pan and cook the meatballs in two batches until lightly browned all over.

6 Lift the meatballs out with a slotted spoon and drain on kitchen paper.

7 Pour the sauce into a tagine or an ovenproof casserole dish. Top with the meatballs, cover and cook in the preheated oven for 25–30 minutes, or until the meatballs are cooked through and the sauce is bubbling. Garnish with freshly chopped herbs and serve immediately on a bed of couscous or plain boiled rice.

Nutritional details per 100 g energy 94 kcals/394 kj · protein 12 g · carbohydrate 8 g · fat 2 g · fibre 0.5 g · sugar 1.7 g · sodium trace

✓ cows' milk-free   ✓ egg-free   ◖ gluten-free   ◖ wheat-free   ✓ nut-free   ◖ vegetarian   ◖ vegan   ✓ seafood-free

2

4

7

Zesty Whole-baked Fish

INGREDIENTS

Serves 4

1.8 kg/4 lb whole salmon, cleaned
freshly ground black pepper
50 g/2 oz low-fat spread
1 garlic clove, peeled and
  finely sliced
zest and juice of 1 lemon
zest of 1 orange
1 tsp freshly grated nutmeg
3 tbsp Dijon mustard
2 tbsp fresh white breadcrumbs
2 bunches fresh dill
1 bunch fresh tarragon
1 lime sliced
150 ml/¼ pint half-fat crème fraîche
450 ml/¾ pint fromage frais
dill sprigs, to garnish

1 Preheat the oven to 220°C/425°F/Gas Mark 7. Lightly rinse the fish and pat dry with absorbent kitchen paper. Season the cavity with a little pepper. Make several diagonal cuts across the flesh of the fish and season.

2 Mix together the low-fat spread, garlic, lemon and orange zest and juice, nutmeg, mustard and fresh breadcrumbs. Mix well together. Spoon the breadcrumb mixture into the slits with a small sprig of dill. Place the remaining herbs inside the fish cavity. Weigh the fish and calculate the cooking time – allow 10 minutes per 450 g/1 lb.

3 Lay the fish onto a double thickness of tinfoil. If liked, smear the fish with a little low fat spread. Top with the lime slices and fold the foil into a parcel. Chill in the refrigerator for about 15 minutes.

4 Place in a roasting tin and cook in the preheated oven for the calculated cooking time. Fifteen minutes before the end of cooking, open the foil and return until the skin begins to crisp. Remove the fish from the oven and stand for 10 minutes.

5 Pour the juices from the roasting tin into a saucepan. Bring to the boil and stir in the crème fraîche and fromage frais. Simmer for 3 minutes or until hot. Garnish with dill sprigs and serve immediately.

Nutritional details per 100 g   energy 193 kcals/805 kj · protein 21 g · carbohydrate 2 g · fat 12 g · fibre 0.1 g · sugar 0.4 g · sodium 0.2 g

◖ cows' milk-free   ✓ egg-free   ◖ gluten-free   ◖ wheat-free   ✓ nut-free   ◖ vegetarian   ◖ vegan   ◖ seafood-free

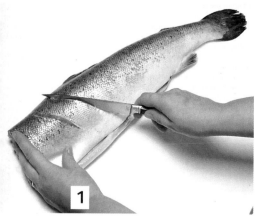

Allergy Free

Food allergies and food intolerances can trigger a whole range of unpleasant symptoms. This section includes recipes that help you to avoid some of the more common allergens such as nuts, cows' milk, egg whites, gluten, berries, Soya beans and fish & shellfish. If you suspect that you have a food allergy it is important that you get tested so that you can use the recipes that avoid this particular food.

Chilli Roast Chicken

INGREDIENTS

Serves 4

3 medium-hot fresh red
  chillies, deseeded
½ tsp ground turmeric
1 tsp cumin seeds
1 tsp coriander seeds
2 garlic cloves, peeled and crushed
2.5 cm/1 inch piece fresh root ginger,
  peeled and chopped
1 tbsp lemon juice
1 tbsp olive oil
2 tbsp roughly chopped
  fresh coriander
½ tsp salt
freshly ground black pepper
1.4 kg/3 lb oven-ready chicken
15 g/½ oz dairy-free
  margarine, melted
550 g/1¼ lb butternut squash
fresh parsley and coriander sprigs,
  to garnish

To serve:

4 baked potatoes
seasonal green vegetables

1   Preheat the oven to 190°C/375°F/Gas Mark 5. Roughly chop the chillies and put in a food processor with the turmeric, cumin seeds, coriander seeds, garlic, ginger, lemon juice, olive oil, coriander, salt, pepper and 2 tablespoons of cold water. Blend to a paste, leaving the ingredients still slightly chunky.

2   Starting at the neck end of the chicken, gently ease up the skin to loosen it from the breast. Reserve 3 tablespoons of the paste. Push the remaining paste over the chicken breast under the skin, spreading it evenly.

3   Put the chicken into a large roasting tin. Mix the reserved chilli paste with the melted margarine. Brush 1 tablespoon of it evenly over the chicken and roast in the preheated oven for 20 minutes.

4   Meanwhile, halve, peel and scoop out the seeds from the butternut squash. Cut into large chunks and mix in the remaining chilli paste and margarine mixture.

5   Arrange the butternut squash around the chicken. Roast for a further hour, basting with the cooking juices about every 20 minutes until the chicken is fully cooked and the squash tender. Garnish with parsley and coriander. Serve hot with baked potatoes and green vegetables.

Nutritional details per 100 g   energy 168 kcals/704 kj · protein 16 g · carbohydrate 4 g · fat 10 g · fibre 0.02 g · sugar 0.02 g · sodium 0.1 g

✓ cows' milk-free   ✓ egg-free   ✓ gluten-free   ✓ wheat-free   ✓ nut-free   ◐ vegetarian   ◯ vegan   ✓ seafood-free

1

2

4

Chinese–glazed Poussin with Green & Black Rice

INGREDIENTS

Serves 4

4 oven-ready poussins
salt and freshly ground black pepper
300 ml/½ pint apple juice
1 cinnamon stick
2 star anise
½ tsp Chinese five-spice powder
50 g/2 oz dark muscovado sugar
2 tbsp tomato purée
1 tbsp cider vinegar
grated rind of 1 orange
350 g/12 oz mixed basmati and
  wild rice
125 g/4 oz mangetout, finely
  sliced lengthways
1 bunch spring onions, trimmed and
  finely shredded lengthways
salt and freshly ground black pepper

1 Preheat the oven to 200°C/400°F/Gas Mark 6, 15 minutes before cooking. Rinse the poussins inside and out and pat dry with absorbent kitchen paper. Using tweezers, remove any feathers. Season well with salt and pepper, then reserve.

2 Pour the apple juice into a small saucepan and add the cinnamon stick, star anise and Chinese five-spice powder. Bring to the boil, then simmer rapidly until reduced by half. Reduce the heat, stir in the sugar, tomato purée, vinegar and orange rind and simmer gently until the sugar is dissolved and the glaze is syrupy. Remove from the heat and leave to cool completely. Remove the whole spices.

3 Place the poussins on a wire rack set over a tinfoil-lined roasting tin. Brush generously with the apple glaze. Roast in the preheated oven for 40–45 minutes, or until the juices run clear when the thigh is pierced with a skewer, basting once or twice with the remaining glaze. Remove the poussins from the oven and leave to cool slightly.

4 Meanwhile, cook the rice according to the packet instructions. Bring a large saucepan of lightly salted water to the boil and add the mangetout. Blanch for 1 minute, then drain thoroughly. As soon as the rice is cooked, drain and transfer to a warmed bowl. Add the mangetout and spring onions, season to taste and stir well. Arrange on warmed dinner plates, place a poussin on top and serve immediately.

Nutritional details per 100 g   energy 178 kcals/744 kj · protein 17 g · carbohydrate 6 g · fat 9 g · fibre 0.2 g · sugar 2 g · sodium 0.08 g

✓ cows' milk-free   ✓ egg-free   ✓ gluten-free   ✓ wheat-free   ✓ nut-free   ○ vegetarian   ○ vegan   ✓ seafood-free

2

3

4

Chinese Leaf & Mushroom Soup

INGREDIENTS

Serves 4–6

450 g/1 lb Chinese leaves

25 g/1 oz dried Chinese
(shiitake) mushrooms

1 tbsp vegetable oil

75 g/3 oz smoked streaky
bacon, diced

2.5 cm/1 inch piece fresh root ginger,
peeled and finely chopped

175 g/6 oz chestnut mushrooms,
thinly sliced

1.1 litres/2 pints gluten-free
chicken stock

4–6 spring onions, trimmed and
cut into short lengths

2 tbsp dry sherry or Chinese rice wine

salt and freshly ground black pepper

sesame oil for drizzling

1   Trim the stem ends of the Chinese leaves and cut in half lengthways. Remove the triangular core with a knife, then cut into 2.5 cm/1 inch slices and reserve.

2   Place the dried Chinese mushrooms in a bowl and pour over enough almost-boiling water to cover. Leave to stand for 20 minutes to soften, then gently lift out and squeeze out the liquid. Discard the stems and thinly slice the caps and reserve. Strain the liquid through a muslin-lined sieve or a coffee filter paper and reserve.

3   Heat a wok over a medium-high heat, add the oil and when hot add the bacon. Stir-fry for 3–4 minutes, or until crisp and golden, stirring frequently. Add the ginger and chestnut mushrooms and stir-fry for a further 2–3 minutes.

4   Add the chicken stock and bring to the boil, skimming off any fat and scum that rises to the surface. Add the spring onions, sherry or rice wine, Chinese leaves, sliced Chinese mushrooms and season to taste with salt and pepper. Pour in the reserved soaking liquid and reduce the heat to the lowest possible setting.

5   Simmer gently, covered, until all the vegetables are very tender; this will take about 10 minutes. Add a little water if the liquid has reduced too much. Spoon into soup bowls and drizzle with a little sesame oil. Serve immediately.

Nutritional details per 100 g   energy 72 kcals/297 kj · protein 4 g · carbohydrate 4 g · fat 5 g · fibre 0.09 g · sugar 0.6 g · sodium 0.55 g

✓ cows' milk-free   ✓ egg-free   ✓ gluten-free   ✓ wheat-free   ✓ nut-free   ◐ vegetarian   ○ vegan   ✓ seafood-free

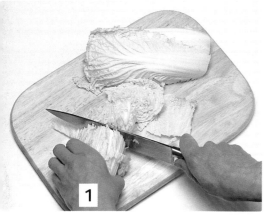

Coconut–baked Courgettes

INGREDIENTS

Serves 4

3 tbsp sunflower oil

1 onion, peeled and
  finely sliced

4 garlic cloves, peeled
  and crushed

½ tsp chilli powder

1 tsp ground coriander

6–8 tbsp desiccated coconut

1 tbsp tomato purée

700 g/1½ lb courgettes,
  thinly sliced

freshly chopped parsley,
  to garnish

1 Preheat the oven to 180°C/350°F/Gas Mark 4, 10 minutes before cooking. Lightly oil a 1.4 litre/2½ pint ovenproof gratin dish. Heat a wok, add the oil and when hot, add the onion and stir-fry for 2–3 minutes. Add the garlic, chilli powder and coriander and stir-fry for 1–2 minutes.

2 Pour 300 ml/½ pint cold water into the wok and bring to the boil. Add the coconut and tomato purée and simmer for 3–4 minutes; most of the water will evaporate at this stage. Spoon 4 tablespoons of the spice and coconut mixture into a small bowl and reserve.

3 Stir the courgettes into the remaining spice and coconut mixture and spoon into the oiled gratin dish. Sprinkle the reserved spice and coconut mixture evenly over the top. Bake, uncovered, in the preheated oven for 15–20 minutes, or until golden. Garnish with chopped parsley and serve.

Please note that coconut is fine for most nut allergy sufferers, but please check with your doctor if you have any concerns.

Nutritional details per 100 g   energy 112 kcals/468 kj · protein 3 g · carbohydrate 4 g · fat 10 g · fibre 2 g · sugar 3 g · sodium trace

✓ cows' milk-free   ✓ egg-free   ✓ gluten-free   ✓ wheat-free   ✓ nut-free   ✓ vegetarian   ✓ vegan   ✓ seafood-free

Coconut Chicken Soup

INGREDIENTS

Serves 4

2 lemon grass stalks

3 tbsp vegetable oil

3 medium onions, peeled and
   finely sliced

3 garlic cloves, peeled
   and crushed

2 tbsp fresh root ginger,
   finely grated

2–3 kaffir lime leaves

1½ tsp turmeric

1 red pepper, deseeded and diced

400 ml can coconut milk

1.1 litres/2 pints gluten-free vegetable
   or chicken stock

275 g/9 oz easy-cook long-grain rice

275 g/10 oz cooked chicken meat

285 g can sweetcorn, drained

3 tbsp freshly chopped coriander

freshly chopped pickled chillies,
   to serve

1 Discard the outer leaves of the lemon grass stalks, then place onto a chopping board and, using a mallet or rolling pin, pound gently to bruise and reserve.

2 Heat the vegetable oil in a large saucepan and cook the onions over a medium heat for about 10–15 minutes until soft and beginning to change colour.

3 Lower the heat, stir in the garlic, ginger, lime leaves and turmeric and cook for 1 minute. Add the red pepper, coconut milk, stock, lemon grass and rice. Bring to the boil, cover and simmer gently over a low heat for about 10 minutes.

4 Cut the chicken into bite-sized pieces, then stir into the soup, with the sweetcorn and the freshly chopped coriander. Reheat gently, stirring frequently. Serve immediately with a few chopped pickled chillies to sprinkle on top.

Nutritional details per 100 g   energy 121 kcals/510 kj · protein 7 g · carbohydrate 14 g · fat 4 g · fibre 0.7 g · sugar 4.1 g · sodium 0.2 g

✓ cows' milk-free   ✓ egg-free   ✓ gluten-free   ✓ wheat-free   ✓ nut-free   ◖ vegetarian   ◖ vegan   ✓ seafood-free

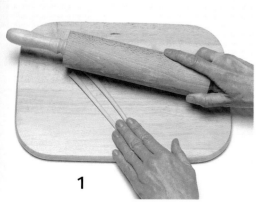

1

3

4

Ginger & Garlic Potatoes

INGREDIENTS

Serves 4

700 g/1½ lb potatoes

2.5 cm/1 inch piece of
  root ginger, peeled and
  coarsely chopped

3 garlic cloves, peeled
  and chopped

½ tsp turmeric

1 tsp salt

5 tbsp vegetable oil

1 tsp whole fennel seeds

1 large eating apple, cored
  and diced

6 spring onions, trimmed
  and sliced diagonally

1 tbsp freshly chopped coriander

To serve:

assorted bitter salad leaves

1   Scrub the potatoes, then place, unpeeled, in a large saucepan and cover with boiling salted water. Bring to the boil and cook for 15 minutes, then drain and leave the potatoes to cool completely. Peel and cut into 2.5 cm/1 inch cubes.

2   Place the root ginger, garlic, turmeric and salt in a food processor and blend for 1 minute. With the motor still running, slowly add 3 tablespoons of water and blend into a paste. Alternatively, pound the ingredients to a paste with a pestle and mortar.

3   Heat the oil in a large heavy-based frying pan and when hot, but not smoking, add the fennel seeds and fry for a few minutes. Stir in the ginger paste and cook for 2 minutes, stirring frequently. Take care not to burn the mixture.

4   Reduce the heat, then add the potatoes and cook for 5–7 minutes, stirring frequently, until the potatoes have a golden-brown crust. Add the diced apple and spring onions, then sprinkle with the freshly chopped coriander. Heat through for 2 minutes, then serve on assorted salad leaves.

Nutritional details per 100 g   energy 116 kcals/487 kj · protein 2 g · carbohydrate 15 g · fat 6 g · fibre 1 g · sugar 0.7 g · sodium 0.2 g

✓ cows' milk-free   ✓ egg-free   ✓ gluten-free   ✓ wheat-free   ✓ nut-free   ✓ vegetarian   ✓ vegan   ✓ seafood-free

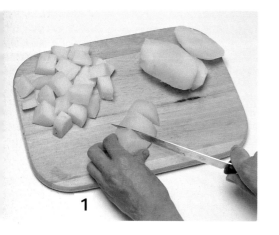

1   2   4

Hot & Spicy Red Cabbage with Apples

INGREDIENTS

Serves 8

900 g/2 lb red cabbage,
  cored and shredded
450 g/1 lb onions, peeled
  and finely sliced
450 g/1 lb cooking apples, peeled,
  cored and finely sliced
½ tsp mixed spice
1 tsp ground cinnamon
2 tbsp light soft brown sugar
salt and freshly ground
  black pepper
grated rind of 1 large orange
1 tbsp fresh orange juice
50 ml/2 fl oz medium sweet
  cider (or apple juice)
2 tbsp wine vinegar

To serve:

dairy-free yogurt
freshly ground black pepper

1. Preheat the oven to 150°C/300°F/Gas Mark 2. Put just enough cabbage in a large casserole dish to cover the base evenly.

2. Place a layer of the onions and apples on top of the cabbage.

3. Sprinkle a little of the mixed spice, cinnamon and sugar over the top. Season with salt and pepper.

4. Spoon over a small portion of the orange rind, orange juice and the cider.

5. Continue to layer the casserole dish with the ingredients in the same order until used up.

6. Pour the vinegar as evenly as possible over the top layer of the ingredients.

7. Cover the casserole dish with a close-fitting lid and bake in the preheated oven, stirring occasionally, for 2 hours until the cabbage is moist and tender. Serve immediately with the dairy-free yogurt and black pepper.

Nutritional details per 100 g   energy 42 kcals/176 kj · protein 1 g · carbohydrate 8 g · fat 0.6 g · fibre 0.4 g · sugar 5 g · sodium trace

✓ cows' milk-free   ✓ egg-free   ✓ gluten-free   ✓ wheat-free   ✓ nut-free   ✓ vegetarian   ✓ vegan   ✓ seafood-free

2

4

5

Meatballs with Bean & Tomato Sauce

INGREDIENTS

Serves 4

1 large onion, peeled and
   finely chopped

1 red pepper, deseeded
   and chopped

1 tbsp freshly chopped oregano

½ tsp hot paprika

425 g can red kidney
   beans, drained

300 g/11 oz fresh beef mince

salt and freshly ground
   black pepper

4 tbsp sunflower oil

1 garlic clove, peeled
   and crushed

400 g can chopped tomatoes

1 tbsp freshly chopped coriander,
   to garnish

freshly cooked rice,
   to serve

1 Make the meatballs by blending half the onion, half the red pepper, the oregano, the paprika and 350 g/12 oz of the kidney beans in a blender or food processor for a few seconds. Add the beef with some seasoning and blend until well mixed. Turn the mixture onto a lightly floured board and form into small balls.

2 Heat the wok, then add 2 tablespoons of the oil and, when hot, stir-fry the meatballs gently until well browned on all sides. Remove with a slotted spoon and keep warm.

3 Wipe the wok clean, then add the remaining oil and cook the remaining onion and pepper and the garlic for 3–4 minutes, until soft. Add the tomatoes, seasoning to taste and remaining kidney beans.

4 Return the meatballs to the wok, stir them into the sauce, then cover and simmer for 10 minutes. Sprinkle with the chopped coriander and serve immediately with the freshly cooked rice.

Nutritional details per 100 g energy 112 kcals/471 kj · protein 6 g · carbohydrate 12 g · fat 5 g · fibre 2 g · sugar 3 g · sodium 0.1 g

✓ cows' milk-free   ✓ egg-free   ◖ gluten-free   ✓ wheat-free   ✓ nut-free   ◖ vegetarian   ◖ vegan   ✓ seafood-free

1

2

4

Mediterranean Rice Salad

INGREDIENTS

Serves 4

250 g/9 oz Camargue red rice
2 sun-dried tomatoes, finely chopped
2 garlic cloves, peeled and
   finely chopped
4 tbsp oil from a jar of
   sun-dried tomatoes
2 tsp balsamic vinegar
2 tsp red wine vinegar
salt and freshly ground black pepper
1 red onion, peeled and thinly sliced
1 yellow pepper, quartered
   and deseeded
1 red pepper, quartered and deseeded
½ cucumber, peeled and diced
6 ripe plum tomatoes,
   cut into wedges
1 fennel bulb, halved and thinly sliced
fresh basil leaves, to garnish

1   Cook the rice in a saucepan of lightly salted boiling water for 35–40 minutes, or until tender. Drain well and reserve.

2   Whisk the sun-dried tomatoes, garlic, oil and vinegars together in a small bowl or jug. Season to taste with salt and pepper. Put the red onion in a large bowl, pour over the dressing and leave to allow the flavours to develop.

3   Put the peppers, skin-side up, on a grill rack and cook under a preheated hot grill for 5–6 minutes, or until blackened and charred. Remove and place in a plastic bag. When cool enough to handle, peel off the skins and slice the peppers.

4   Add the peppers, cucumber, tomatoes, fennel and rice to the onions. Mix gently together to coat in the dressing. Cover and chill in the refrigerator for 30 minutes to allow the flavours to mingle.

5   Remove the salad from the refrigerator and leave to stand at room temperature for 20 minutes. Garnish with fresh basil leaves and serve.

Nutritional details per 100 g   energy 48 kcals/202 kj · protein 1 g · carbohydrate 9 g · fat 1 g · fibre trace · sugar trace · sodium trace

✓ cows' milk-free   ✓ egg-free   ✓ gluten-free   ✓ wheat-free   ✓ nut-free   ✓ vegetarian   ✓ vegan   ✓ seafood-free

2

3

4

Oven–baked Pork Balls with Peppers

INGREDIENTS

Serves 4

450 g/1 lb fresh pork mince
4 tbsp freshly chopped basil
2 garlic cloves, peeled
  and chopped
3 sun-dried tomatoes, chopped
salt and freshly ground black pepper
3 tbsp olive oil
1 medium red pepper, deseeded
  and cut into chunks
1 medium green pepper, deseeded
  and cut into chunks
1 medium yellow pepper, deseeded
  and cut into chunks
225 g/8 oz cherry tomatoes
2 tbsp balsamic vinegar

1 Preheat oven to 200°C/400°F/Gas Mark 6, 15 minutes before cooking.

2 Mix together the pork, basil, 1 chopped garlic clove, sun-dried tomatoes and seasoning until well combined.

3 With damp hands, divide the mixture into 16 equal portions, then roll into balls and reserve.

4 Spoon the olive oil into a large roasting tin and place in the preheated oven for about 3 minutes, until very hot.

5 Remove from the heat and stir in the pork balls, the remaining chopped garlic and peppers. Bake for about 15 minutes.

6 Remove from the oven and stir in the cherry tomatoes and season to taste with plenty of salt and pepper. Bake for about a further 20 minutes.

7 Remove the pork balls from the oven, stir in the vinegar and serve immediately.

Nutritional details per 100 g   energy 139 kcals/582 kj · protein 8 g · carbohydrate 5 g · fat 10 g · fibre 0.5 g · sugar 1 g · sodium 0.2 g

✓ cows' milk-free   ✓ egg-free   ✓ gluten-free   ✓ wheat-free   ✓ nut-free   ◖ vegetarian   ◖ vegan   ✓ seafood-free

2

3

6

Sweet Potato Crisps with Mango Salsa

INGREDIENTS

Serves 6

For the salsa:
1 large, ripe mango, peeled, stoned
  and cut into small cubes
8 cherry tomatoes, quartered
½ cucumber, peeled if preferred
  and finely diced
1 red onion, peeled and
  finely chopped
pinch of sugar
1 red chilli, deseeded and
  finely chopped
2 tbsp rice vinegar
2 tbsp olive oil
grated rind and juice of 1 lime

450 g/1 lb sweet potatoes,
  peeled and thinly sliced
vegetable oil, for deep frying
sea salt
2 tbsp freshly chopped mint

1 To make the salsa, mix the mango with the tomatoes, cucumber and onion. Add the sugar, chilli, vinegar, oil and the lime rind and juice. Mix together thoroughly, cover and leave for 45–50 minutes.

2 Soak the potatoes in cold water for 40 minutes to remove as much of the excess starch as possible. Drain and dry thoroughly in a clean tea towel, or absorbent kitchen paper.

3 Heat the oil to 190°C/375°F in a deep fryer. When at the correct temperature, place half the potatoes in the frying basket, then carefully lower the potatoes into the hot oil and cook for 4–5 minutes, or until they are golden brown, shaking the basket every minute so that they do not stick together.

4 Drain the potato crisps on absorbent kitchen paper, sprinkle with sea salt and place under a preheated moderate grill for a few seconds to dry out. Repeat with the remaining potatoes. Stir the mint into the salsa and serve with the potato crisps.

Nutritional details per 100 g   energy 141 kcals/582 kj · protein 1 g · carbohydrate 13 g · fat 10 g · fibre 0.5 g · sugar 0.2 g · sodium 0.2 g

✓ cows' milk-free   ✓ egg-free   ✓ gluten-free   ✓ wheat-free   ✓ nut-free   ✓ vegetarian   ✓ vegan   ✓ seafood-free

1

3

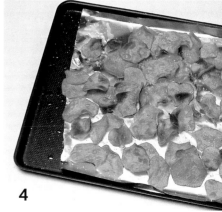

4

Venetian Herb Orzo

INGREDIENTS

Serves 4–6

200 g/7 oz baby spinach leaves
150 g/5 oz rocket leaves
50 g/2 oz flat leaf parsley
6 spring onions, trimmed
few leaves of fresh mint
3 tbsp extra virgin olive oil,
  plus more if required
450 g/11 oz orzo
salt and freshly ground black pepper

1. Rinse the spinach leaves in several changes of cold water and reserve. Finely chop the rocket leaves with the parsley and mint. Thinly slice the green of the spring onions.

2. Bring a large saucepan of water to the boil, add the spinach leaves, herbs and spring onions and cook for about 10 seconds. Remove and rinse under cold running water. Drain well and, using your hands, squeeze out all the excess moisture.

3. Place the spinach, herbs and spring onions in a food processor. Blend for 1 minute then, with the motor running, gradually pour in the olive oil until the sauce is well blended.

4. Meanwhile, bring a large pan of lightly salted water to a rolling boil. Add the pasta and cook according to the packet instructions, or until 'al dente'. Drain thoroughly and place in a large warmed bowl.

5. Add the spinach sauce to the orzo and stir lightly until the orzo is well coated. Stir in an extra tablespoon of olive oil if the mixture seems too thick. Season well with salt and pepper. Serve immediately on warmed plates or allow to cool to room temperature.

Nutritional details per 100 g   energy 121 kcals/505 kj · protein 2 g · carbohydrate 17 g · fat 5 g · fibre 1 g · sugar 0.5 g · sodium trace

✓ cows' milk-free   ✓ egg-free   ◐ gluten-free   ◐ wheat-free   ✓ nut-free   ✓ vegetarian   ✓ vegan   ✓ seafood-free

1

3

5

Warm Chicken & Potato Salad with Peas & Mint

INGREDIENTS

Serves 4–6

450 g/1 lb new potatoes,
  peeled or scrubbed and
  cut into bite-sized pieces
salt and freshly ground
  black pepper
2 tbsp cider vinegar
175 g/6 oz frozen garden peas, thawed
1 small ripe avocado
4 cooked chicken breasts,
  about 450 g/1 lb in weight, skinned
  and diced
2 tbsp freshly chopped mint
2 heads Little Gem lettuce
fresh mint sprigs, to garnish

For the dressing:

2 tbsp raspberry or sherry vinegar
2 tsp gluten-free Dijon mustard
1 tsp clear honey
50 ml/2 fl oz sunflower oil
50 ml/2 fl oz extra virgin olive oil

1. Cook the potatoes in lightly salted boiling water for 15 minutes, or until just tender when pierced with the tip of a sharp knife; do not overcook. Rinse under cold running water to cool slightly, then drain and turn into a large bowl. Sprinkle with the cider vinegar and toss gently.

2. Run the peas under hot water to ensure that they are thawed, pat dry with absorbent kitchen paper and add to the potatoes.

3. Cut the avocado in half lengthways and remove the stone. Peel and cut the avocado into cubes and add to the potatoes and peas. Add the chicken and stir together lightly.

4. To make the dressing, place all the ingredients in a screw-top jar with a little salt and pepper, and shake well to mix; add a little more oil if the flavour is too sharp. Pour over the salad and toss gently to coat. Sprinkle in half the mint and stir lightly.

5. Separate the lettuce leaves and spread onto a large shallow serving plate. Spoon the salad on top and sprinkle with the remaining mint. Garnish with mint sprigs and serve.

Nutritional details per 100 g   energy 138 kcals/577 kj · protein 12 g · carbohydrate 8 g · fat 7 g · fibre 1 g · sugar 1 g · sodium trace

✓ cows' milk-free   ✓ egg-free   ◖ gluten-free   ✓ wheat-free   ✓ nut-free   ◖ vegetarian   ◖ vegan   ✓ seafood-free

1

3

4

Wheat & Gluten Free

Living with intolerance to wheat and gluten need not be difficult if you manage to replace this important complex carbohydrate with other fibre-rich foods. This section provides enticing recipes that avoid foods which contain wheat and gluten, and offer a healthy alternative.

Aubergine & Yogurt Dip

INGREDIENTS

Makes 600 ml/1 pint

2 x 225 g/8 oz aubergines
1 tbsp light olive oil
1 tbsp lemon juice
2 garlic cloves, peeled and crushed
190 g jar pimentos, drained
150 ml¼ pint low-fat
  natural yogurt
salt and freshly ground black pepper
25 g/1 oz black olives,
  pitted and chopped
225 g/8 oz cauliflower florets
225 g/8 oz broccoli florets
125 g/4 oz carrots, peeled and
  cut into 5 cm/2 inch strips

1 Preheat the oven to 200°C/400°F/Gas Mark 6. Pierce the skin of the aubergines with a fork and place on a baking tray. Cook for 40 minutes or until very soft.

2 Cool the aubergines, then cut in half, scoop out the flesh, and tip into a bowl.

3 Mash the aubergine with the olive oil, lemon juice and garlic until smooth or blend for a few seconds in a food processor.

4 Chop the pimentos finely and add to the aubergine mixture.

5 When blended add the yogurt. Stir well and season to taste with salt and pepper.

6 Add the chopped olives and leave in the refrigerator to chill for at least 30 minutes.

7 Place the cauliflower and broccoli florets and carrot strips into a pan and cover with boiling water. Simmer for 2 minutes, then rinse in cold water. Drain and serve as crudités to accompany the dip.

Nutritional details per 100 g   energy 36 kcals/150 kj · protein 2 g · carbohydrate 5 g · fat 1 g · fibre 0.7 g · sugar 1.4 g · sodium trace

◖ cows' milk-free   ✓ egg-free   ✓ gluten-free   ✓ wheat-free   ✓ nut-free   ✓ vegetarian   ◖ vegan   ✓ seafood-free

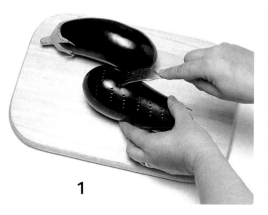

1

3

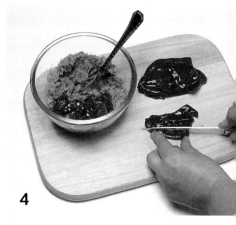

4

Baby Roast Potato Salad

INGREDIENTS

Serves 4

350 g/12 oz small shallots
sea salt and freshly ground
  black pepper
900 g/2 lb small, even-sized
  new potatoes
2 tbsp olive oil
2 medium courgettes
2 sprigs of fresh rosemary
175 g/6 oz cherry tomatoes
150 ml/¼ pint soured cream
2 tbsp freshly snipped chives
¼ tsp paprika

1 Preheat the oven to 200°C/400°F/Gas Mark 6. Trim the shallots, but leave the skins on. Put into a saucepan of lightly salted boiling water along with the potatoes and cook for 5 minutes and drain. Separate the shallots and plunge them into cold water for 1 minute.

2 Put the oil in a baking sheet lined with tinfoil or roasting tin and heat for a few minutes. Peel the skins off the shallots – they should now come away easily. Add to the baking sheet or roasting tin with the potatoes and toss in the oil to coat. Sprinkle with a little sea salt. Roast the potatoes and shallots in the preheated oven for 10 minutes.

3 Meanwhile, trim the courgettes, halve lengthways and cut into 5 cm/2 inch chunks. Add to the baking sheet or roasting tin, toss to mix and cook for 5 minutes.

4 Pierce the tomato skins with a sharp knife. Add to the sheet or tin with the rosemary and cook for a further 5 minutes, or until all the vegetables are tender. Remove the rosemary and discard. Grind a little black pepper over the vegetables.

5 Spoon into a wide serving bowl. Mix together the soured cream, paprika and chives and drizzle over the vegetables just before serving.

Nutritional details per 100 g   energy 68 kcals/286 kj · protein 2 g · carbohydrate 9 g · fat 3 g · fibre 1.1 g · sugar 1.6 g · sodium trace

cows' milk-free   ✓ egg-free   ✓ gluten-free   ✓ wheat-free   ✓ nut-free   ✓ vegetarian   vegan   ✓ seafood-free

1

3

4

Carrot & Parsnip Terrine

INGREDIENTS

Serves 8–10

550 g/1¼ lb carrots,
  peeled and chopped
450 g/1 lb parsnips,
  peeled and chopped
6 tbsp half-fat crème fraîche
450 g/1 lb spinach, rinsed
1 tbsp brown sugar
1 tbsp freshly chopped parsley
½ tsp freshly grated nutmeg
salt and freshly ground black pepper
6 medium eggs
sprigs of fresh basil, to garnish

For the tomato coulis:

450 g/1 lb ripe tomatoes,
  deseeded and chopped
1 medium onion, peeled and
  finely chopped

1. Preheat the oven to 200°C/400°F/Gas Mark 6. Oil and line a 900 g/ 2 lb loaf tin with non-stick baking paper. Cook the carrots and parsnips in boiling salted water for 10–15 minutes or until very tender. Drain and purée separately. Add 2 tablespoons of crème fraîche to both the carrots and the parsnips.

2. Steam the spinach for 5–10 minutes or until very tender. Drain and squeeze out as much liquid as possible, then stir in the remaining crème fraîche.

3. Add the brown sugar to the carrot purée, the parsley to the parsnip mixture and the nutmeg to the spinach. Season all three to taste with salt and pepper.

4. Beat 2 eggs, add to the spinach and turn into the prepared tin. Add another 2 beaten eggs to the carrot mixture and layer carefully on top of the spinach. Beat the remaining eggs into the parsnip purée and layer on top of the terrine.

5. Place the tin in a baking dish and pour in enough hot water to come halfway up the sides of the tin. Bake in the preheated oven for 1 hour until a skewer inserted into the centre comes out clean. Leave to cool for at least 30 minutes. Run a sharp knife around the edges. Turn out on to a dish and reserve.

6. Make the tomato coulis by simmering the tomatoes and onions together for 5–10 minutes until slightly thickened. Season to taste. Blend well in a liquidiser or food processor and serve as an accompaniment to the terrine. Garnish with sprigs of basil and serve.

Nutritional details per 100 g energy 49 kcals/206 kj · protein 3 g · carbohydrate 6 g · fat 2 g · fibre 2.2 g · sugar 4.2 g · sodium trace

cows' milk-free · egg-free · ✓ gluten-free · ✓ wheat-free · ✓ nut-free · ✓ vegetarian · vegan · ✓ seafood-free

3

4

6

Chicken & Seafood Risotto

INGREDIENTS

Serves 6–9

125 ml/4 fl oz olive oil

1.4 kg/3 lb chicken, cut into 8 pieces

350 g/12 oz spicy chorizo sausage,
  cut into 1 cm/½ inch pieces

125 g/4 oz cured ham, diced

1 onion, peeled and chopped

2 red or yellow peppers, deseeded
  and cut into 2.5 cm/1 inch pieces

4 garlic cloves, peeled and
  finely chopped

750 g/1 lb 10 oz short-grain Spanish
  rice or Arborio rice

2 bay leaves

1 tsp dried thyme

1 tsp saffron strands, lightly crushed

200 ml/7 fl oz dry white wine

1.6 litres/2¾ pints gluten-free
  chicken stock

salt and freshly ground black pepper

125 g/4 oz fresh shelled peas

450 g/1 lb uncooked prawns

36 clams and/or mussels,
  well scrubbed

2 tbsp freshly chopped parsley

fresh parsley sprigs, to garnish

1 Heat half the oil in a 45.5 cm/18 inch paella pan or deep, wide frying pan. Add the chicken pieces and fry for 15 minutes, turning constantly, until golden. Remove from the pan and reserve. Add the chorizo and ham to the pan and cook for 6 minutes until crisp, stirring occasionally. Remove and add to the chicken.

2 Add the onion to the pan and cook for 3 minutes until beginning to soften. Add the peppers and garlic and cook for 2 minutes, then add to the reserved chicken, chorizo and ham.

3 Add the remaining oil to the pan and stir in the rice until well coated. Stir in the bay leaves, thyme and saffron, then pour in the wine and bubble until evaporated, stirring and scraping up any bits on the bottom of the pan. Stir in the stock and bring to the boil, stirring occasionally.

4 Return the chicken, chorizo, ham and vegetables to the pan, burying them gently in the rice. Season to taste with salt and pepper. Reduce the heat and simmer for 10 minutes, stirring occasionally.

5 Add the peas and seafood, pushing them gently into the rice. Cover, cook over a low heat for 5 minutes, or until the rice and prawns are tender and the clams and mussels open – discard any that do not open. Stand for 5 minutes. Sprinkle with the parsley and serve.

Nutritional details per 100 g energy 152 kcals/638 kj · protein 17 g · carbohydrate 7 g · fat 6 g · fibre 0.3 g · sugar 0.8 g · sodium 0.5 g

✓ cows' milk-free   ✓ egg-free   ✓ gluten-free   ✓ wheat-free   ✓ nut-free   ◖ vegetarian   ◖ vegan   ◖ seafood-free

1

3

5

Coconut Seafood

INGREDIENTS

Serves 4

2 tbsp sunflower oil

450 g/1 lb raw king prawns, peeled

2 bunches spring onions,
  trimmed and thickly sliced

1 garlic clove, peeled
  and chopped

2.5 cm/1 inch piece fresh root ginger,
  peeled and cut into matchsticks

125 g/4 oz fresh shiitake mushrooms,
  rinsed and halved

150 ml/¼ pint dry white wine

200 ml/7 fl oz carton
  coconut cream

4 tbsp freshly chopped coriander

salt and freshly ground
  black pepper

freshly cooked fragrant Thai rice

1 Heat a large wok, add the oil and heat until it is almost smoking, swirling the oil around the wok to coat the sides. Add the prawns and stir-fry over a high heat for 4–5 minutes, or until browned on all sides. Using a slotted spoon, transfer the prawns to a plate and keep warm in a low oven.

2 Add the spring onions, garlic and ginger to the wok and stir-fry for 1 minute. Add the mushrooms and stir-fry for a further 3 minutes. Using a slotted spoon, transfer the mushroom mixture to a plate and keep warm in a low oven.

3 Add the wine and coconut cream to the wok, bring to the boil and boil rapidly for 4 minutes, until reduced slightly.

4 Return the mushroom mixture and prawns to the wok, bring back to the boil, then simmer for 1 minute, stirring occasionally, until piping hot. Stir in the freshly chopped coriander and season to taste with salt and pepper. Serve immediately with the freshly cooked fragrant Thai rice.

Nutritional details per 100 g   energy 125 kcals/527 kj · protein 8 g · carbohydrate 12 g · fat 5 g · fibre 0.2 g · sugar 0.3 g · sodium 0.5 g

✓ cows' milk-free   ✓ egg-free   ✓ gluten-free   ✓ wheat-free   ✓ nut-free   ◖ vegetarian   ◖ vegan   ◖ seafood-free

Crown Roast of Lamb

INGREDIENTS

Serves 6

1 lamb crown roast
salt and freshly ground black pepper
1 tbsp sunflower oil
1 small onion, peeled and
  finely chopped
2–3 garlic cloves, peeled and crushed
2 celery stalks, trimmed and
  finely chopped
125 g/4 oz cooked mixed basmati
  and wild rice
75 g/3 oz ready-to-eat-dried
  apricots, chopped
50 g/2 oz pine nuts, toasted
1 tbsp finely grated orange rind
2 tbsp freshly chopped coriander
1 small egg, beaten
freshly roasted potatoes and
  green vegetables, to serve

1. Preheat the oven to 180°C/350°F/Gas Mark 4, about 10 minutes before roasting. Wipe the crown roast and season the cavity with salt and pepper. Place in a roasting tin and cover the ends of the bones with small pieces of tinfoil.

2. Heat the oil in a small saucepan and cook the onion, garlic and celery for 5 minutes, then remove the saucepan from the heat. Add the cooked rice with the apricots, pine nuts, orange rind and coriander. Season with salt and pepper, then stir in the egg and mix well.

3. Carefully spoon the prepared stuffing into the cavity of the lamb, then roast in the preheated oven for 1–1 ½ hours. Remove the lamb from the oven and remove and discard the tinfoil from the bones. Return to the oven and continue to cook for a further 15 minutes, or until cooked to personal preference.

4. Remove from the oven and leave to rest for 10 minutes before serving with the roast potatoes and freshly cooked vegetables.

Nutritional details per 100 g   energy 147 kcals/617 kj · protein 6 g · carbohydrate 17 g · fat 7 g · fibre 2 g · sugar 2.7 g · sodium trace

✓ cows' milk-free   ◖ egg-free   ✓ gluten-free   ✓ wheat-free   ◖ nut-free   ◖ vegetarian   ◖ vegan   ✓ seafood-free

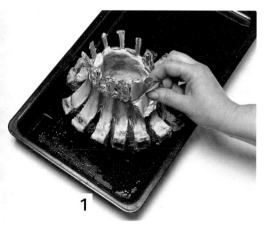

1

2

3

Fresh Tuna Salad

INGREDIENTS

Serves 4

225 g/8 oz mixed salad leaves
225 g/8 oz baby cherry tomatoes,
  halved lengthways
125 g/4 oz rocket leaves, washed
2 tbsp olive oil
550 g/1¼ lb boned tuna steaks, each
  cut into 4 small pieces
50 g/2 oz piece fresh
  Parmesan cheese

For the dressing:

8 tbsp olive oil
grated zest and juice of
  2 small lemons
1 tbsp gluten-free
  wholegrain mustard
salt and freshly ground
  black pepper

1 Wash the salad leaves and place in a large salad bowl with the cherry tomatoes and rocket and reserve.

2 Heat the wok, then add the oil and heat until almost smoking. Add the tuna, skin-side down, and cook for 4–6 minutes, turning once during cooking, or until cooked and the flesh flakes easily. Remove from the heat and leave to stand in the juices for 2 minutes before removing.

3 Meanwhile, make the dressing. Place the olive oil, lemon zest and juices and mustard in a small bowl or screw-topped jar and whisk or shake until well blended. Season to taste with salt and pepper.

4 Transfer the tuna to a clean chopping board and flake, then add it to the salad and toss lightly.

5 Using a swivel blade vegetable peeler, peel the piece of Parmesan cheese into shavings. Divide the salad between four large serving plates, drizzle the dressing over the salad, then scatter with the Parmesan shavings.

Nutritional details per 100 g   energy 156 kcals/646 kj · protein 13 g · carbohydrate 3 g · fat 8 g · fibre 0.1 g · sugar 0.2 g · sodium trace

● cows' milk-free   ✓ egg-free   ✓ gluten-free   ✓ wheat-free   ✓ nut-free   ● vegetarian   ● vegan   ● seafood-free

2

3

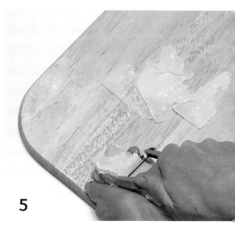

5

Pumpkin & Smoked Haddock Soup

INGREDIENTS

Serves 4–6

2 tbsp olive oil

1 medium onion, peeled
   and chopped

2 garlic cloves, peeled
   and chopped

3 celery stalks, trimmed
   and chopped

700 g/1½ lb pumpkin, peeled,
   deseeded and cut into chunks

450 g/1 lb potatoes, peeled and
   cut into chunks

750 ml/1¼ pints gluten-free chicken
   stock, heated

125 ml/4 fl oz dry sherry

200 g/7 oz smoked haddock fillet

150 ml/¼ pint milk

freshly ground black pepper

2 tbsp freshly chopped parsley

1 Heat the oil in a large heavy-based saucepan and gently cook the onion, garlic and celery for about 10 minutes. This will release the sweetness but not colour the vegetables. Add the pumpkin and potatoes to the saucepan and stir to coat the vegetables with the oil.

2 Gradually pour in the stock and bring to the boil. Cover, then reduce the heat and simmer for 25 minutes, stirring occasionally. Stir in the dry sherry, then remove the saucepan from the heat and leave to cool for 5–10 minutes.

3 Blend the mixture in a food processor or blender to form a chunky purée and return to the saucepan.

4 Meanwhile, place the fish in a shallow frying pan. Pour in the milk with 3 tablespoons of water and bring to almost boiling point. Reduce the heat, cover, and simmer for 6 minutes, or until the fish is cooked and flakes easily. Remove from the heat and, using a slotted spoon, remove the fish from the liquid, reserving both liquid and fish.

5 Discard the skin and any bones from the fish and flake into pieces. Stir the fish liquid into the soup, together with the flaked fish. Season with freshly ground black pepper, stir in the parsley and serve immediately.

Nutritional details per 100 g   energy 58 kcals/246 kj · protein 4 g · carbohydrate 6 g · fat 1.7 g · fibre 0.9 g · sugar 1.8 g · sodium 0.3 g

◖ cows' milk-free   ✓ egg-free   ✓ gluten-free   ✓ wheat-free   ✓ nut-free   ◖ vegetarian   ◖ vegan   ◖ seafood-free

1

4

5

Seared Scallop Salad

INGREDIENTS

Serves 4

12 king (large) scallops
1 tbsp butter
2 tbsp orange juice
2 tbsp balsamic vinegar
1 tbsp clear honey
2 ripe pears, washed
125 g/4 oz rocket
125 g/4 oz watercress
50 g/2 oz walnuts
freshly ground black pepper

1. Clean the scallops, removing the thin black vein from around the white meat and coral. Rinse thoroughly and dry on absorbent kitchen paper.

2. Cut into 2–3 thick slices, depending on the scallop size.

3. Heat a griddle pan or heavy-based frying pan, then when hot, add the butter and allow to melt.

4. Once melted, sear the scallops for 1 minute on each side or until golden. Remove from the pan and reserve.

5. Briskly whisk together the orange juice, balsamic vinegar and honey to make the dressing and reserve.

6. With a small, sharp knife carefully cut the pears into quarters, core then cut into chunks.

7. Mix the rocket leaves, watercress, pear chunks and walnuts. Pile onto serving plates and top with the scallops.

8. Drizzle over the dressing and grind over plenty of black pepper. Serve immediately.

Nutritional details per 100 g   energy 116 kcals/483 kj · protein 6 g · carbohydrate 8 g · fat 6 g · fibre 1.4 g · sugar 6.1 g · sodium 0.1 g

◐ cows' milk-free   ✓ egg-free   ✓ gluten-free   ✓ wheat-free   ◐ nut-free   ◐ vegetarian   ◐ vegan   ◐ seafood-free

1

4

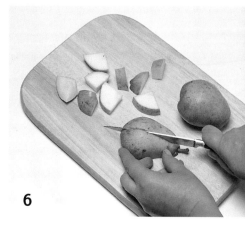

6

Special Rosti

INGREDIENTS

Serves 4

700 g/1½ lb potatoes,
   scrubbed but not peeled
salt and freshly ground
   black pepper
75 g/3 oz butter
1 large onion, peeled and
   finely chopped
1 garlic clove, peeled and crushed
2 tbsp freshly chopped parsley
1 tbsp olive oil
75 g/3 oz Parma ham,
   thinly sliced
50 g/2 oz sun-dried
   tomatoes, chopped
175 g/ 6 oz Emmenthal
   cheese, grated
mixed green salad, to serve

1   Cook the potatoes in a large saucepan of salted boiling water for about 10 minutes, until just tender. Drain in a colander, then rinse in cold water. Drain again. Leave until cool enough to handle, then peel off the skins.

2   Melt the butter in a large frying pan and gently fry the onion and garlic for about 3 minutes until softened and beginning to colour. Remove from the heat.

3   Coarsely grate the potatoes into a large bowl, then stir in the onion and garlic mixture. Sprinkle over the parsley and stir well to mix. Season to taste with salt and pepper.

4   Heat the oil in the frying pan and cover the base of the pan with half the potato mixture. Lay the slices of Parma ham on top. Sprinkle with the chopped sun-dried tomatoes, then scatter the grated Emmenthal over the top.

5   Finally, top with the remaining potato mixture. Cook over a low heat, pressing down with a palette knife from time to time, for 10–15 minutes, or until the bottom is golden brown. Carefully invert the rosti onto a large plate, then carefully slide back into the pan and cook the other side until golden. Serve cut into wedges with a mixed green salad.

Nutritional details per 100 g   energy 147 kcals/611 kj · protein 5 g · carbohydrate 11 g · fat 9 g · fibre 0.9 g · sugar 1.5 g · sodium 0.2 g

◖ cows' milk-free   ✓ egg-free   ✓ gluten-free   ✓ wheat-free   ✓ nut-free   ◖ vegetarian   ◖ vegan   ✓ seafood-free

3   4   5

Spiced Indian Roast Potatoes with Chicken

INGREDIENTS

Serves 4

700 g/1½ lb waxy potatoes, peeled
  and cut into large chunks
salt and freshly ground
  black pepper
4 tbsp sunflower oil
8 chicken drumsticks
1 large Spanish onion, peeled
  and roughly chopped
3 shallots, peeled and
  roughly chopped
2 large garlic cloves, peeled
  and crushed
1 red chilli
2 tsp fresh root ginger,
  peeled and finely grated
2 tsp ground cumin
2 tsp ground coriander
pinch of cayenne pepper
4 cardamom pods, crushed
sprigs of fresh coriander,
  to garnish

1 Preheat the oven to 190°C/375°F/Gas Mark 5, about 10 minutes before cooking. Parboil the potatoes for 5 minutes in lightly salted boiling water, then drain thoroughly and reserve. Heat the oil in a large frying pan, add the chicken drumsticks and cook until sealed on all sides. Remove and reserve.

2 Add the onions and shallots to the pan and fry for 4–5 minutes, or until softened. Stir in the garlic, chilli and ginger and cook for 1 minute, stirring constantly. Stir in the ground cumin, coriander, cayenne pepper and crushed cardamom pods and continue to cook, stirring, for a further minute.

3 Add the potatoes to the pan, then add the chicken. Season to taste with salt and pepper. Stir gently until the potatoes and chicken pieces are coated in the onion and spice mixture.

4 Spoon into a large roasting tin and roast in the preheated oven for 35 minutes, or until the chicken and potatoes are cooked thoroughly. Garnish with fresh coriander and serve immediately.

Nutritional details per 100 g energy 142 kcals/598 kj · protein 9 g · carbohydrate 14 g · fat 5 g · fibre 1.2 g · sugar 1.3 g · sodium trace

✓ cows' milk-free   ✓ egg-free   ✓ gluten-free   ✓ wheat-free   ✓ nut-free   ◐ vegetarian   ◐ vegan   ✓ seafood-free

Almond Macaroons

INGREDIENTS

Makes 12

rice paper
125 g/4 oz caster sugar
50 g/2 oz ground almonds
1 tsp ground rice
2–3 drops almond essence
1 medium egg white
8 blanched almonds, halved

1 Preheat the oven to 150°C/300°F/Gas Mark 2, 10 minutes before baking. Line a baking sheet with the rice paper.

2 Mix the caster sugar, ground almonds, ground rice and almond essence together and reserve.

3 Whisk the egg white until stiff then gently fold in the caster sugar mixture with a metal spoon or rubber spatula.

4 Mix to form a stiff but not sticky paste. If the mixture is very sticky, add a little extra ground almonds.

5 Place small spoonfuls of the mixture, about the size of an apricot, well apart on the rice paper.

6 Place a half-blanched almond in the centre of each. Place in the preheated oven and bake for 25 minutes, or until just pale golden.

7 Remove the biscuits from the oven and leave to cool for a few minutes on the baking sheet. Cut or tear the rice paper around the macaroons to release them. Once cold, serve or otherwise store them in an airtight tin.

Nutritional details per 100 g energy 383 kcals/1621 kj · protein 5 g · carbohydrate 72 g · fat 10 g · fibre trace · sugar 58 g · sodium trace

✓ cows' milk-free   egg-free   ✓ gluten-free   ✓ wheat-free   nut-free   ✓ vegetarian   vegan   ✓ seafood-free

2

4

6

Chocolate Mousse Cake

INGREDIENTS

Cuts into 8–10 servings

For the cake:

450 g/1 lb plain dark
 chocolate, chopped

125 g/4 oz butter, softened

3 tbsp brandy

9 large eggs, separated

150 g/5 oz caster sugar

For the chocolate glaze:

225 ml/8 fl oz double cream

225 g/8 oz plain dark
 chocolate, chopped

2 tbsp brandy

1 tbsp single cream and white
 chocolate curls, to decorate

1   Preheat the oven to 180°C/350°F/Gas Mark 4, 10 minutes before baking. Lightly oil and line the bases of two 20.5 cm/8 inch springform tins with baking paper. Melt the chocolate and butter in a bowl set over a saucepan of simmering water. Stir until smooth. Remove from the heat and stir in the brandy.

2   Whisk the egg yolks and the sugar, reserving 2 tablespoons of the sugar, until thick and creamy. Slowly beat in the chocolate mixture until smooth. Whisk the egg whites until soft peaks form, then sprinkle over the remaining sugar and continue whisking until stiff.

3   Fold a large spoonful of the egg whites into the chocolate mixture. Gently fold in the remaining egg whites. Divide about two thirds of the mixture evenly between the tins. Reserve the remaining one third of the chocolate mousse mixture for the filling. Bake in the preheated oven for about 20 minutes, or until well risen and set. Remove and cool for at least 1 hour.

4   Loosen the edges of the cake layers and, using your fingertips, lightly press the crusty edges down. Pour the rest of the mousse over one layer. Carefully unclip the side, remove the other cake from the tin and gently invert onto the mousse, bottom side up. Discard the lining paper and chill for 4–6 hours, or until set.

5   To make the glaze, melt the cream and chocolate with the brandy in a saucepan and stir until smooth. Cool until thickened. Unclip the side of the mousse cake and place on a wire rack. Spread over half the glaze. Allow to set, then decorate with chocolate curls. To serve, heat the remaining glaze and pour round each slice, and dot with cream.

Nutritional details per 100 g   energy 407 kcals/1699 kj · protein 6 g · carbohydrate 36 g · fat 26 g · fibre 1 g · sugar 35 g · sodium trace

◖ cows' milk-free   ◖ egg-free   ✓ gluten-free   ✓ wheat-free   ✓ nut-free   ✓ vegetarian   ◖ vegan   ✓ seafood-free

1

2

4

White Chocolate Terrine with Red Fruit Compote

INGREDIENTS

Serves 8

225 g/8 oz white chocolate
300 ml/½ pint double cream
225 g/8 oz full-fat soft cream cheese
2 tbsp finely grated orange rind
125 g/4 oz caster sugar
350 g/12 oz mixed summer
   fruits, such as strawberries,
   blueberries and raspberries
1 tbsp Cointreau
sprigs of fresh mint, to decorate

1. Set the freezer to rapid freeze at least 2 hours before required. Lightly oil and line a 450 g/1 lb loaf tin with clingfilm, taking care to keep the clingfilm as wrinkle free as possible. Break the white chocolate into small pieces and place in a heatproof bowl set over a saucepan of gently simmering water. Leave for 20 minutes or until melted, then remove from the heat and stir until smooth. Leave to cool.

2. Whip the cream until soft peaks form. Beat the cream cheese until soft and creamy, then beat in the grated orange rind and 50 g/2 oz of the caster sugar. Mix well, then fold in the whipped cream and then the cooled, melted white chocolate.

3. Spoon the mixture into the prepared loaf tin and level the surface. Place in the freezer and freeze for at least 4 hours or until frozen. Once frozen, remember to return the freezer to its normal setting.

4. Place the fruits with the remaining sugar in a heavy-based saucepan and heat gently, stirring occasionally, until the sugar has dissolved and the juices from the fruits are just beginning to run. Add the Cointreau.

5. Dip the loaf tin into hot water for 30 seconds and invert onto a serving plate. Carefully remove the tin and clingfilm. Decorate with sprigs of mint and serve sliced with the red fruit compote.

Nutritional details per 100 g   energy 345 kcals/1432 kj · protein 3 g · carbohydrate 24 g · fat 27 g · fibre 0.3 g · sugar 22 g · sodium trace

◖ cows' milk-free   ✓ egg-free   ◖ gluten-free   ✓ wheat-free   ✓ nut-free   ◖ vegetarian   ◖ vegan   ✓ seafood-free

2

3

4

Dairy Free

Dairy foods can contain a high amount of cholesterol and saturated fat. Eating foods that avoid dairy is not just for those who are lactose intolerant but those wishing to follow a healthier lifestyle. The meals in this section offer nutritious and delicious alternatives to meals that include dairy, which will help you to lead such a lifestyle.

Aromatic Duck Burgers on Potato Pancakes

INGREDIENTS

Serves 4

700 g/1½ lb boneless duck breasts

2 tbsp hoisin sauce

1 garlic clove, peeled and
    finely chopped

4 spring onions, trimmed and
    finely chopped

2 tbsp Japanese soy sauce

½ tsp Chinese five-spice powder

salt and freshly ground black pepper

freshly chopped coriander, to garnish

extra hoisin sauce, to serve

For the potato pancakes:

450 g/1 lb floury potatoes

1 small onion, peeled and grated

1 small egg, beaten

1 heaped tbsp plain flour

1 Peel off the thick layer of fat from the duck breasts and cut into small pieces. Put the fat into a small dry saucepan and set over a low heat for 10–15 minutes, or until the fat runs clear.

2 Cut the duck meat into pieces and blend in a food processor until coarsely chopped. Spoon into a bowl and add the hoisin sauce, garlic, half the spring onions, soy sauce and Chinese five-spice powder. Season to taste with salt and pepper and shape into four burgers. Cover and chill in the refrigerator for 1 hour.

3 To make the potato pancakes, grate the potatoes into a large bowl, squeeze out the water with your hands, then put on a clean tea towel and twist the ends to squeeze out any remaining water. Return the potato to the bowl, add the onion and egg and mix well. Add the flour and salt and pepper. Stir to blend.

4 Heat about 2 tablespoons of the clear duck fat in a large frying pan. Spoon the potato mixture into 2–4 pattie shapes and cook for 6 minutes, or until golden and crisp, turning once. Keep warm in the oven. Repeat with the remaining mixture, adding duck fat as needed.

5 Preheat the grill and line the grill rack with tinfoil. Brush the burgers with a little of the duck fat and grill for 6–8 minutes, or longer if wished, turning once. Arrange 1–2 potato pancakes on a plate and top with a burger. Spoon over a little hoisin sauce and garnish with the remaining spring onions and coriander.

Nutritional details per 100 g   energy 162 kcals/677 kj · protein 15 g · carbohydrate 7 g · fat 8 g · fibre 0.2 g · sugar 0.5 g · sodium 0.4 g

✓ cows' milk-free   egg-free   gluten-free   wheat-free   ✓ nut-free   vegetarian   vegan   ✓ seafood-free

1

3

4

Barbecued Fish Kebabs

INGREDIENTS

Serves 4

450 g/1 lb herring or mackerel fillets,
   cut into chunks
2 small red onions, quartered
16 cherry tomatoes
salt and freshly ground black pepper
freshly cooked couscous, to serve

For the sauce:

150 ml/¼ pint fish stock
5 tbsp tomato ketchup
2 tbsp Worcestershire sauce
2 tbsp wine vinegar
2 tbsp brown sugar
2 drops Tabasco
2 tbsp tomato purée

1 Line a grill rack with a single layer of tinfoil and preheat the grill at a high temperature, 2 minutes before use.

2 If using wooden skewers, soak in cold water for 30 minutes to prevent them from catching alight during cooking.

3 Meanwhile, prepare the sauce. Add the fish stock, tomato ketchup, Worcestershire sauce, vinegar, sugar, Tabasco and tomato purée to a small saucepan. Stir well and leave to simmer for 5 minutes.

4 When ready to cook, drain the skewers, if necessary, then thread the fish chunks, the quartered red onions and the cherry tomatoes alternately on to the skewers.

5 Season the kebabs to taste with salt and pepper and brush with the sauce. Grill under the preheated grill for 8–10 minutes, basting with the sauce occasionally during cooking. Turn the kebabs often to ensure that they are cooked thoroughly and evenly on all sides. Serve immediately with couscous.

Nutritional details per 100 g energy 116 kcals/486 kj · protein 9 g · carbohydrate 9 g · fat 5 g · fibre 0.3 g · sugar 7.4 g · sodium 0.3 g

✓ cows' milk-free   ✓ egg-free   ◐ gluten-free   ◐ wheat-free   ✓ nut-free   ◐ vegetarian   ◐ vegan   ◐ seafood-free

3

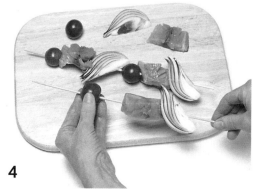

4

5

Braised Chicken in Beer

INGREDIENTS

Serves 4

4 chicken joints, skinned
125 g/4 oz pitted dried prunes
2 bay leaves
12 shallots
2 tsp olive oil
125 g/4 oz small button
  mushrooms, wiped
1 tsp soft dark brown sugar
½ tsp wholegrain mustard
2 tsp tomato purée
150 ml/¼ pint light ale
150 ml/¼ pint chicken stock
salt and freshly ground
  black pepper
2 tsp cornflour
2 tsp lemon juice
2 tbsp chopped fresh parsley
flat-leaf parsley, to garnish

To serve:

mashed potatoes
seasonal green vegetables

1 Preheat the oven to 170°C/325°F/Gas Mark 3. Cut each chicken joint in half and put in an ovenproof casserole dish with the prunes and bay leaves.

2 To peel the shallots, put in a small bowl and cover with boiling water.

3 Drain the shallots after 2 minutes and rinse under cold water until cool enough to handle. The skins should then peel away easily from the shallots.

4 Heat the oil in a large, non-stick frying pan. Add the shallots and gently cook for about 5 minutes until beginning to colour. Add the mushrooms to the pan and cook for a further 3–4 minutes until both the mushrooms and onions are softened.

5 Sprinkle the sugar over the shallots and mushrooms, then add the mustard, tomato purée, ale and chicken stock. Season to taste with salt and pepper and bring to the boil, stirring to combine. Carefully pour over the chicken.

6 Cover the casserole dish and cook in the preheated oven for 1 hour. Blend the cornflour with the lemon juice and 1 tablespoon of cold water and stir into the casserole. Return to the oven for a further 10 minutes or until the chicken is cooked and the vegetables are tender.

7 Remove the bay leaves and stir in the chopped parsley. Garnish the chicken with the flat-leaf parsley. Serve with the mashed potatoes and fresh green vegetables.

Nutritional details per 100 g   energy 89 kcals/377 kj · protein 10 g · carbohydrate 8 g · fat 2 g · fibre 1.6 g · sugar 4.3 g · sodium 0.1 g

✓ cows' milk-free   ✓ egg-free   ◐ gluten-free   ◐ wheat-free   ✓ nut-free   ◐ vegetarian   ◐ vegan   ✓ seafood-free

1

4

5

Coconut Fish Curry

INGREDIENTS

Serves 4

2 tbsp sunflower oil

1 medium onion, peeled and very
  finely chopped

1 yellow pepper, deseeded and
  finely chopped

1 garlic clove, peeled and crushed

1 tbsp mild curry paste

2.5 cm/1 inch piece of root ginger,
  peeled and grated

1 red chilli, deseeded and
  finely chopped

400 ml can coconut milk

700 g/1½ lb firm white fish,
  e.g. monkfish fillets, skinned
  and cut into chunks

225 g/8 oz basmati rice

1 tbsp freshly chopped coriander

1 tbsp mango chutney

salt and freshly ground black pepper

To serve:

lime wedges

fresh coriander sprigs

Greek yogurt made from ewe's milk

warm naan bread

1 Put 1 tablespoon of the oil into a large frying pan and cook the onion, pepper and garlic for 5 minutes, or until soft. Add the remaining oil, curry paste, ginger and chilli and cook for a further minute.

2 Pour in the coconut milk and bring to the boil, reduce the heat and simmer gently for 5 minutes, stirring occasionally. Add the monkfish to the pan and continue to simmer gently for 5–10 minutes, or until the fish is tender, but not overcooked.

3 Meanwhile, cook the rice in a saucepan of boiling salted water for 15 minutes, or until tender. Drain the rice thoroughly and turn out into a serving dish.

4 Stir the chopped coriander and chutney gently into the fish curry and season to taste with salt and pepper. Spoon the fish curry over the cooked rice, garnish with lime wedges and coriander sprigs and serve immediately with spoonfuls of Greek yogurt (avoid if intolerant of ewe's milk) and warm naan bread.

Nutritional details per 100 g   energy 139 kcals/583 kj · protein 9 g · carbohydrate 19 g · fat 3 g · fibre 0.4 g · sugar 2.6 g · sodium 0.2 g

✓ cows' milk-free   ✓ egg-free   ● gluten-free   ● wheat-free   ✓ nut-free   ● vegetarian   ● vegan   ● seafood-free

Courgette & Tarragon Tortilla

INGREDIENTS

Serves 6

700 g/1½ lb potatoes
3 tbsp olive oil
1 onion, peeled and thinly sliced
salt and freshly ground
  black pepper
1 courgette, trimmed and
  thinly sliced
6 medium eggs
2 tbsp freshly chopped tarragon
tomato wedges, to serve

1. Peel the potatoes and thinly slice. Dry the slices in a clean tea towel to get them as dry as possible. Heat the oil in a large heavy-based pan, add the onion and cook for 3 minutes. Add the potatoes with a little salt and pepper, then stir the potatoes and onion lightly to coat in the oil.

2. Reduce the heat to the lowest possible setting, cover and cook gently for 5 minutes. Turn the potatoes and onion over and continue to cook for a further 5 minutes. Give the pan a shake every now and again to ensure that the potatoes do not stick to the base or burn. Add the courgette, then cover and cook for a further 10 minutes.

3. Beat the eggs and tarragon together and season to taste with salt and pepper. Pour the egg mixture over the vegetables and return to the heat. Cook on a low heat for up to 20–25 minutes, or until there is no liquid egg left on the surface of the tortilla.

4. Turn the tortilla over by inverting it onto the lid or onto a flat plate. Return the pan to the heat and cook for a final 3–5 minutes, or until the underside is golden brown. If preferred, place the tortilla under a preheated grill for 4 minutes, or until set and golden brown on top. Cut into small squares and serve hot or cold with tomato wedges.

Nutritional details per 100 g   energy 118 kcals/496 kj · protein 4 g · carbohydrate 15 g · fat 5 g · fibre 1.3 g · sugar 1.5 g · sodium trace
✓ cows' milk-free   egg-free   ✓ gluten-free   ✓ wheat-free   ✓ nut-free   ✓ vegetarian   vegan   ✓ seafood-free

Haddock with an Olive Crust

INGREDIENTS

Serves 4

12 pitted black olives, finely chopped
75 g/3 oz fresh white breadcrumbs
1 tbsp freshly chopped tarragon
1 garlic clove, peeled and crushed
3 spring onions, trimmed and
   finely chopped
1 tbsp olive oil
4 x 175 g/6 oz thick skinless
   haddock fillets

To serve:
freshly cooked carrots
freshly cooked beans

1 Preheat the oven to 190°C/375°F/Gas Mark 5. Place the black olives in a small bowl with the breadcrumbs and add the chopped tarragon.

2 Add the garlic to the olives with the chopped spring onions and the olive oil. Mix together lightly.

3 Wipe the fillets with either a clean damp cloth or damp kitchen paper, then place on a lightly oiled baking sheet.

4 Place spoonfuls of the olive and breadcrumb mixture on top of each fillet and press the mixture down lightly and evenly over the top of the fish.

5 Bake the fish in the preheated oven for 20–25 minutes or until the fish is cooked thoroughly and the topping is golden brown. Serve immediately with the freshly cooked carrots and beans.

Nutritional details per 100 g   energy 93 kcals/394 kj • protein 13 g • carbohydrate 6 g • fat 2 g • fibre 1.2 g • sugar 1.1 g • sodium 0.2 g

✓ cows' milk-free   ✓ egg-free   ◖ gluten-free   ◖ wheat-free   ✓ nut-free   ◖ vegetarian   ◖ vegan   ◖ seafood-free

2

3

4

Hoisin Chicken Pancakes

INGREDIENTS

Serves 4

3 tbsp hoisin sauce
1 garlic clove, peeled and crushed
2.5 cm/1 inch piece root ginger,
  peeled and finely grated
1 tbsp soy sauce
1 tsp sesame oil
salt and freshly ground black pepper
4 skinless chicken thighs
½ cucumber, peeled (optional)
12 bought Chinese pancakes
6 spring onions, trimmed and cut
  lengthways into fine shreds
sweet chilli dipping sauce,
  to serve

1 Preheat the oven to 190°C/375°F/Gas Mark 5. In a non-metallic bowl, mix the hoisin sauce with the garlic, ginger, soy sauce, sesame oil and seasoning.

2 Add the chicken thighs and turn to coat in the mixture. Cover loosely and leave in the refrigerator to marinate for 3–4 hours, turning the chicken from time to time.

3 Remove the chicken from the marinade and place in a roasting tin. Reserve the marinade. Bake in the preheated oven for 30 minutes, basting occasionally with the marinade.

4 Cut the cucumber in half lengthways and remove the seeds by running a teaspoon down the middle to scoop them out. Cut into thin batons.

5 Place the pancakes in a steamer to warm or heat according to packet instructions. Thinly slice the hot chicken and arrange on a plate with the shredded spring onions, cucumber and pancakes.

6 Place a spoonful of the chicken in the middle of each warmed pancake and top with pieces of cucumber, spring onion, and a little dipping sauce. Roll up and serve immediately.

Nutritional details per 100 g   energy 184 kcals/780 kj   ·   protein 21 g   ·   carbohydrate 21 g   ·   fat 2 g   ·   fibre 0.8 g   ·   sugar 0.7 g   ·   sodium 0.4 g

✓ cows' milk-free   ✓ egg-free   ◖ gluten-free   ◖ wheat-free   ✓ nut-free   ◖ vegetarian   ◖ vegan   ✓ seafood-free

2

4

5

Pan-cooked Chicken with Thai Spices

INGREDIENTS

Serves 4

4 kaffir lime leaves
5 cm/2 inch piece of root ginger,
  peeled and chopped
300 ml/½ pint chicken
  stock, boiling
4 x 175 g/6 oz chicken breasts
2 tsp groundnut oil
5 tbsp coconut milk
1 tbsp fish sauce
2 red chillies, deseeded and
  finely chopped
225 g/8 oz Thai jasmine rice
1 tbsp lime juice
3 tbsp freshly chopped coriander
salt and freshly ground
  black pepper

To garnish:
wedges of lime
freshly chopped coriander

1 Lightly bruise the kaffir lime leaves and put into a bowl with the chopped ginger. Pour over the chicken stock, cover and leave to infuse for 30 minutes.

2 Meanwhile, cut each chicken breast into two pieces. Heat the oil in a large, non-stick frying pan or flameproof casserole dish and brown the chicken pieces for 2–3 minutes on each side.

3 Strain the infused chicken stock into the pan. Half cover the pan with a lid and gently simmer for 10 minutes.

4 Stir in the coconut milk, fish sauce and chopped chillies. Simmer, uncovered for 5–6 minutes, or until the chicken is tender and cooked through and the sauce has reduced slightly.

5 Meanwhile, cook the rice in boiling salted water according to the packet instructions. Drain the rice thoroughly.

6 Stir the lime juice and chopped coriander into the sauce. Season to taste with salt and pepper. Serve the chicken and sauce on a bed of rice. Garnish with wedges of lime and freshly chopped coriander and serve immediately.

Nutritional details per 100 g energy 133 kcals/560 kj · protein 21 g · carbohydrate 8 g · fat 2 g · fibre 0.4 g · sugar trace · sodium 0.3 g

✓ cows' milk-free ✓ egg-free ◖ gluten-free ◖ wheat-free ◖ nut-free ◖ vegetarian ◖ vegan ◖ seafood-free

1

2

4

Prawn & Chilli Soup

INGREDIENTS

Serves 4

2 spring onions, trimmed
225 g/8 oz whole raw tiger prawns
750 ml/1¼ pint fish stock
finely grated rind and juice of 1 lime
1 tbsp fish sauce
1 red chilli, deseeded and chopped
1 tbsp soy sauce
1 lemon grass stalk
2 tbsp rice vinegar
4 tbsp freshly chopped coriander

1 To make spring onion curls, finely shred the spring onions lengthways. Place in a bowl of iced cold water and reserve.

2 Remove the heads and shells from the prawns leaving the tails intact.

3 Split the prawns almost in two to form a butterfly shape and individually remove the black thread that runs down the back of each one.

4 In a large pan heat the stock with the lime rind and juice, fish sauce, chilli and soy sauce.

5 Bruise the lemon grass by crushing it along its length with a rolling pin, then add to the stock mixture.

6 When the stock mixture is boiling add the prawns and cook until they are pink.

7 Remove the lemon grass and add the rice vinegar and coriander.

8 Ladle into bowls and garnish with the spring onion curls. Serve immediately.

Nutritional details per 100 g energy 72 kcals/304 kj · protein 13 g · carbohydrate 4 g · fat 1 g · fibre trace · sugar 0.5 g · sodium 1.2 g

✓ cows' milk-free   ✓ egg-free   gluten-free   wheat-free   ✓ nut-free   vegetarian   vegan   seafood-free

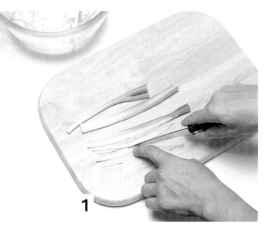

1

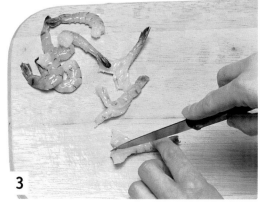

3

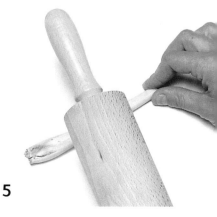

5

Royal Fried Rice

INGREDIENTS

Serves 4

450 g/1 lb Thai fragrant rice
2 large eggs
2 tsp sesame oil
salt and freshly ground black pepper
3 tbsp vegetable oil
1 red pepper, deseeded and
  finely diced
1 yellow pepper, deseeded and
  finely diced
1 green pepper, deseeded and
  finely diced
2 red onions, peeled and diced
125 g/4 oz sweetcorn kernels
125 g/4 oz cooked peeled prawns,
  thawed if frozen
125 g/4 oz white crabmeat,
  drained if canned
¼ tsp sugar
2 tsp light soy sauce

To garnish:
radish roses
freshly snipped and whole
  chive leaves

1 Place the rice in a sieve, rinse with cold water, then drain. Place in a saucepan and add twice the volume of water, stirring briefly. Bring to the boil, cover and simmer gently for 15 minutes without further stirring. If the rice has fully absorbed the water while covered, add a little more water. Continue to simmer, uncovered, for another 5 minutes or until the rice is fully cooked and the water has evaporated. Leave to cool.

2 Place the eggs, sesame oil and a pinch of salt in a small bowl. Using a fork, mix just to break the egg. Reserve.

3 Heat a wok and add 1 tablespoon of the vegetable oil. When very hot, stir-fry the peppers, onion and sweetcorn for 2 minutes or until the onion is soft. Remove the vegetables and reserve.

4 Clean the wok and add the remaining oil. When very hot, add the cold cooked rice and stir-fry for 3 minutes, or until it is heated through. Drizzle in the egg mixture and continue to stir-fry for 2–3 minutes or until the eggs have set.

5 Add the prawns and crabmeat to the rice. Stir-fry for 1 minute. Season to taste with salt and pepper and add the sugar with the soy sauce. Stir to mix and spoon into a warmed serving dish. Garnish with a radish flower and sprinkle with freshly snipped and whole chives. Serve immediately.

Nutritional details per 100 g energy 107 kcals/445 kj · protein 5 g · carbohydrate 13 g · fat 4 g · fibre 0.1 g · sugar 0.9 g · sodium 0.3 g

✓ cows' milk-free   egg-free   gluten-free   wheat-free   ✓ nut-free   vegetarian   vegan   seafood-free

1

3

4

Salmon Teriyaki with Noodles & Crispy Greens

INGREDIENTS

Serves 4

350 g/12 oz salmon fillet
3 tbsp Japanese soy sauce
3 tbsp mirin or sweet sherry
3 tbsp sake
1 tbsp freshly grated root ginger
225 g/8 oz spring greens
vegetable oil for deep-frying
pinch of salt
½ tsp caster sugar
125 g/4 oz flat rice noodles

To garnish:

1 tbsp freshly chopped dill
sprigs of fresh dill
zest of ½ lemon

1. Cut the salmon into paper-thin slices and place in a shallow dish. Mix together the soy sauce, mirin or sherry, sake and the ginger. Pour over the salmon, cover and leave to marinate for 15–30 minutes.

2. Remove and discard the thick stalks from the spring greens. Lay several leaves on top of each other, roll up tightly, then shred finely.

3. Pour in enough oil to cover about 5 cm/2 inches of the wok. Deep-fry the greens in batches for about 1 minute each until crisp. Remove and drain on absorbent kitchen paper. Transfer to a serving dish, sprinkle with salt and sugar and toss together.

4. Place the noodles in a bowl and pour over warm water to cover. Leave to soak for 15–20 minutes until soft, then drain. With scissors cut into 15 cm/6 inch lengths.

5. Remove the salmon slices from the marinade, reserving the marinade for later, and arrange them in a single layer on a baking sheet. Grill for about 2 minutes, until lightly cooked, without turning.

6. When the oil in the wok is cool enough, tip most of it away, leaving about 1 tablespoon behind. Heat until hot, then add the noodles and the reserved marinade and stir-fry for 3–4 minutes. Tip the noodles into a large, warmed serving bowl and arrange the salmon slices on top, garnished with chopped dill, sprigs of fresh dill and lemon zest. Scatter with a little of the crispy greens and serve the rest separately.

Nutritional details per 100 g energy 196 kcals/813 kj · protein 12 g · carbohydrate 6 g · fat 14 g · fibre 0.9 g · sugar 1.5 g · sodium 0.5 g

✓ cows' milk-free   ✓ egg-free   ◖ gluten-free   ◖ wheat-free   ✓ nut-free   ◖ vegetarian   ◖ vegan   ◖ seafood-free

1

2

6

Shredded Beef in Hoisin Sauce

INGREDIENTS

Serves 4

2 celery sticks

125 g/4 oz carrots

450 g/1 lb rump steak

2 tbsp cornflour

salt and freshly ground black pepper

2 tbsp sunflower oil

4 spring onions, trimmed
  and chopped

2 tbsp light soy sauce

1 tbsp hoisin sauce

1 tbsp sweet chilli sauce

2 tbsp dry sherry

250 g pack fine egg thread noodles

1 tbsp freshly chopped coriander

1 Trim the celery and peel the carrots, then cut into fine matchsticks and reserve.

2 Place the steak between two sheets of greaseproof paper or baking parchment. Beat the steak with a meat mallet or rolling pin until very thin, then slice into strips. Season the cornflour with salt and pepper and use to coat the steak. Reserve.

3 Heat a wok, add the oil and when hot, add the spring onions and cook for 1 minute, then add the steak and stir-fry for a further 3–4 minutes, or until the meat is sealed.

4 Add the celery and carrot matchsticks to the wok and stir-fry for a further 2 minutes before adding the soy, hoisin and chilli sauces and the sherry. Bring to the boil and simmer for 2–3 minutes, or until the steak is tender and the vegetables are cooked.

5 Plunge the fine egg noodles into boiling water and leave for 4 minutes. Drain, then spoon onto a large serving dish. Top with the cooked shredded steak, then sprinkle with chopped coriander and serve immediately.

Nutritional details per 100 g   energy 151 kcals/633 kj · protein 14 g · carbohydrate 10 g · fat 6 g · fibre 0.6 g · sugar 1 g · sodium 0.3 g

✓ cows' milk-free   egg-free   gluten-free   wheat-free   ✓ nut-free   vegetarian   vegan   ✓ seafood-free

3

4

4

Sweet-&-Sour Rice with Chicken

INGREDIENTS

Serves 4

4 spring onions
2 tsp sesame oil
1 tsp Chinese five-spice powder
450 g/1 lb chicken breast,
  cut into cubes
1 tbsp vegetable oil
1 garlic clove, peeled and crushed
1 medium onion, peeled and
  sliced into thin wedges
225 g/8 oz long-grain white rice
600 ml/1 pint water
4 tbsp tomato ketchup
1 tbsp tomato purée
2 tbsp honey
1 tbsp vinegar
1 tbsp dark soy sauce
1 carrot, peeled and cut
  into matchsticks

1   Trim the spring onions, then cut lengthways into fine strips. Drop into a large bowl of iced water and reserve.

2   Mix together the sesame oil and Chinese five-spice powder and use to rub into the cubed chicken. Heat the wok, then add the oil and when hot, cook the garlic and onion for 2–3 minutes, or until transparent and softened.

3   Add the chicken and stir-fry over a medium-high heat until the chicken is golden and cooked through. Using a slotted spoon, remove from the wok and keep warm.

4   Stir the rice into the wok and add the water, tomato ketchup, tomato purée, honey, vinegar and soy sauce. Stir well to mix. Bring to the boil, then simmer until almost all of the liquid is absorbed. Stir in the carrot and reserved chicken and continue to cook for 3–4 minutes.

5   Drain the spring onions, which will have become curly. Garnish with the spring onion curls and serve immediately with the rice and chicken.

Nutritional details per 100 g   energy 126 kcals/528 kj · protein 14 g · carbohydrate 12 g · fat 3 g · fibre 0.5 g · sugar 5.7 g · sodium 0.2 g

✓ cows' milk-free   ✓ egg-free   ◖ gluten-free   ◖ wheat-free   ✓ nut-free   ◖ vegetarian   ◖ vegan   ✓ seafood-free

Index